THE S
GUIDE TO
ORGANIC
GARDENING

Bob Sherman
Illustrations by Rob Dalton

COLLINS & BROWN

First published in Great Britain in 1991
by Collins & Brown Limited
Mercury House
195 Knightsbridge
London SW7 1RE

A CIP catalogue record for this book
is available from the British Library

ISBN 1 85585 051 6

Editor Sarah Hoggett
Designed by Ruth Hope and Claire Graham

Phototypeset by Falcon Graphic Art Ltd,
Wallington, Surrey
Printed and bound in Great Britain
by The Bath Press

CONTENTS

ACKNOWLEDGEMENTS

MY FIRST DEBT of gratitude I owe to the late Lawrence Hills, who died recently. Lawrence's pioneering ideas inspired me many years ago to become an organic gardener along with so many others, some of whom are now my colleagues. The society founded by Lawrence Hills to pursue and promote the highest horticultural ideals, The Henry Doubleday Research Association, has now become my employer and has given me the opportunity and background to enable me to write this book. The support and advice of my colleagues at work has contributed greatly to it. Special thanks must be given to Ian Litton and Sarah Hoggett who patiently acted as my gardening "guinea-pigs", rooting through the pages and sniffing out the indigestible parts. Finally I must thank my wife, Christina, who, apart from typing every word in the manuscript and retyping every correction, provided me with tireless encouragement and regular sustenance.

INTRODUCTION

SINCE THE SECOND WORLD WAR, the rapid development of agrochemicals has seemed to offer universal abundance without the help of Mother Nature. The results have indeed been impressive, although not without major repercussions. We now have depleted soils, polluted waters and poisoned air, not helped by the foul effluents of some industrial processes — and millions are still hungry. These problems are compounded by a general loss of habitats as woods disappear under motorways, hedges are ripped out and meadows are "improved" or become housing estates.

It has become increasingly clear that the plight of our beautiful planet is due to a misunderstanding of our own role or status. We have come to consider ourselves as the central governing species, able to organize or re-organize all nature for our personal benefit. This is an ecological and spiritual fallacy: all life is interdependent. This is as true in the garden as it is in the few remaining islands of primeval forest. Care of the environment and careful cultivation are part of the same argument. Most of the deserts of the world were — and are still being – created by bad husbandry. There is no need for us to copy this dismal failure in our own back gardens.

The foundation of all good gardening is healthy soil. A soil that is vibrant with life below will nourish healthy plants so long as we continue to feed it. In nature, little is wasted. The birth and vigour of new plants is made possible by the death of others. Everything is recycled in a closed system that can quite happily accommodate human beings — provided that they observe the simple rules. There is no such cycle in the modern human-organized ecology: dead and living material is burnt, other wastes are pumped into the sea and natural fertility is replaced with man-made fertilizer which adds nothing beneficial to the soil and requires additional energy in its making.

Your garden is home to plants, insects, animals and birds above ground, and billions of microscopic organisms, bacteria, fungi, worms and other creatures below it. You, on the other hand, are a comparatively casual visitor. Who has the greater rights? Sympathetic gardening should allow space for all these creatures and still provide pleasure and food for you. Pests can be controlled without being totally exterminated. Weeds are only as much trouble as you make them in your mind. Simple techniques can keep a garden tidy and respectable. We are fortunate in being able to combine the benefits of technological improvements with the wisdom gained from thousands of years of organic gardening experience.

Gardening is one of the most popular British pastimes. The fact that you are now reading these pages suggests that you, too, are (or soon will be) a fervent tiller of the soil, friend to the worm and fancier of flowers. After fifteen years of happy gardening I am certainly not about to dissuade you or discourage your new enthusiasm.

Despite the frantic pace of modern life, the complex technologies of computers and astral travel, there is a timelessness about the work of the garden that will never change. Each season has its purpose and essence. With skill we can cheat and cajole a little, but plants keep their own time. Working outside on the land keeps you in touch with the natural rhythms that, despite all our capricious conceit and disregard, persist and sustain life. If your own existence is routinely punctuated by tubes, trains or traffic jams, the garden can bring you — literally — back to earth.

The healthful aspects of gardening extend also to the production of food. A vegetable that has only travelled down the garden path to reach the pot or plate is certain to have more vitality — and probably more flavour — than its scrubbed, uniform, pre-packed counterpart from across the country. Vegetables adopt their own shape irrespective of the machine-age expectations of supermarkets, and taste none the worse for having the occasional kink or twist. Growing your own fruit and vegetables organically guarantees you safe food and much pleasure.

In the last five years, organic gardening has gained a respectability that has taken even its long-term proponents by surprise. The ideas and practices at its core are not old-fashioned, although they do owe much to the past and to the countless generations of gardeners who lived with nature because they had no choice. The response to the need for change is encouraging and the grey gloom is giving way to a green bloom. The demand for sound information is growing but there is some confusion, however, about the practice and principles of organic husbandry. In the following chapters I have attempted to explain them in simple terms. Gardeners do not all need to be soil scientists or plant pathologists; and beginners, in particular, need information that is free of jargon and scientific formulae. I have tried to avoid technical terms or, where it is difficult to do so, to define them simply. I have also attempted, in passing, to dispel a few myths. Not all the gardening lore that has been passed down over the well-worn handle of a favourite spade has sound origins.

This book does not set out to be an encyclopaedic exposition of all gardening operations. I have tried instead to cover all the basic principles and practices of organic gardening, leaving out details of growing and tending specific crops. This information is widely available in a host of books, some of which are listed on pages 153-5. Above all, I have tried to make the book practical. Armed with this book and reasonably informative seed packets, the inexperienced gardener or the recent convert to organic gardening should be able to make a start. One garden alone may seem a small contribution to the new 'green' revolution — but after all, all the gardens in Britain combined could make an enormous organic conservation area.

Chapter 1
HAND TOOLS

A GOOD SET OF TOOLS can make gardening infinitely more pleasurable. Ancient rakes with teeth missing, forks with bent tines or weak-necked trowels that buckle under pressure may have saved you money but you will live to curse them for their inadequacy. There are many new, sometimes curious, tools on display in garden centres now, all of which have their uses for futuristic seasoned hands, but over the decades the basic set of tools has changed only in the method of manufacture. The list below describes for beginners the uses of the most important tools. Those marked ★ are the essentials: without them you will find gardening a rather primitive pursuit.

Tools for Working the Soil

★Dibber This is one of those tools which really has only one use but is indispensable for that purpose. You can make your own from a broken spade or fork handle. A dibber needs a hand grip and a shaft about 25 to 30 cm (9 to 12 in) long. Its principle use is for planting leeks. Some gardeners use it as a general planting tool, creating a hole simply by pressing the tool into the ground. This makes a smooth-sided, polished hole and tends to compact the surrounding soil and so is not a good substitute for a trowel.

Hand cultivator Usually three-pronged but also five-pronged, this has strong arrow-shaped teeth which, when pulled through the soil, break up large clods and surface compaction. A hand cultivator is a very useful tool for working the soil before raking, but it is not essential.

Dibber 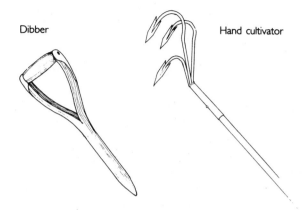 Hand cultivator

★Hand fork This diminutive version of the garden fork is designed for use with one hand.

Uses:

- Digging out weeds
- Harvesting smaller root vegetables
- Breaking up surface crust when working round very tightly planted areas. A good companion for the onion hoe and trowel

★Hoe Traditionally designed hoes are still available but modern creations have added some new ideas to the range. A selection of hoe designs is illustrated on page 10. Some have slightly different uses but all are for slicing off weeds. Of the various types, draw and Dutch hoes are the most useful for beginners.

Draw hoe: The blade is set at right angles to the shaft. It is used with a pulling action.

Uses:

- Weed control
- Making seed drills (see p.60), especially wide drills for peas etc.
- Earthing up potatoes and other crops

Dutch hoe: This tool has a flat blade in the same plane as the shaft and is used with a pushing action. New designs tend to be variations on this traditional idea.

9

Uses:

- Weed control
- Making seed drills
- Breaking up rough surfaces before raking out a seed-bed

Push/pull hoe: A blade front and back allows two goes at the weeds and makes for very precise work round seedlings.

Oscillating hoe: This has a thin, very sharp, double-edged, carbon steel blade which swivels slightly and breaks up the surface soil as well as killing weeds.

Toothed hoe: A drawing action engages the teeth round stems of tougher weeds and pulls them out of the ground.

Onion hoe: A small one-handled hoe with a swan neck. It is useful for precision weeding in tight spots such as a bed of closely spaced onions (hence the name). Appropriate for bed systems (see p.84), it is also useful as a substitute for a trowel when planting out small seedlings.

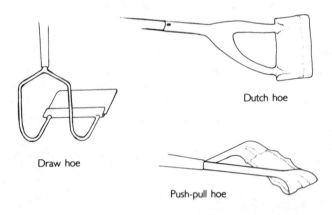

Dutch hoe

Draw hoe

Push-pull hoe

★**Spade** This is such a simple and useful tool that I cannot imagine anyone managing without one. The best spades are well-balanced and should feel light in the hand. If you are over 1.6 m (5 ft 4 in) tall you should try to find one with a handle 86 cm (34 in) long. The standard length is 71 cm (28 in) and it is only recently that longer handles have become available. A handle too short for you is liable to strain your back. Stainless steel spades are regarded with reverence and command a price to match. They will last a lifetime but so should any well-maintained tool. Spades fitted with a tread will save your boots. D- or Y-shaped handles are generally stronger and more comfortable than T-shaped ones but cost a little more.

Spade blades come in two sizes, the smaller being referred to as a border spade. This may well suit those gardeners who are not so strong, as the smaller blade will prevent you from trying to lift too much soil at once. It is designed for use in spaces where a large garden spade might prove clumsy.

Uses:

- Digging
- Trenching
- Planting trees
- Cutting and lifting turf
- Chopping stemmy material for composting
- Trimming lawn edges if you have no edging tool (see p.14)

★**Fork** Possibly the most used tool in the shed. Many of the recommendations given for spades apply also to forks. Again there are two sizes with the smaller — the border fork — being used for work in closely planted areas. Beginners can manage with one fork for all purposes but may well find a use for two sizes within a year or two.

Uses:

- Digging stony soil where a spade jars the wrist
- Loosening compacted soil and breaking up subsoil in double digging
- Working organic matter into the soil
- Harvesting vegetables
- Lifting plants that are to be moved to a new site
- Aerating lawns
- Weeding out deep-rooted and difficult weeds
- Picking up material to load into compost bins

11

★**Garden rake** This tool comes into its own in spring as the seed packets come out of the cupboard. Choose one with a long enough handle to enable you to work with comfort with the teeth at a slightly backward angle. Some rakes have wider heads and, therefore, cover more ground at a time. The garden rake is designed for working soil and thus differs from the *lawn rake* (see p.15).

Uses:

- Creating a smooth, level, fine surface (tilth) for sowing seeds
- Making seed drills (see p.60)
- Scarifying lawns (see p.75)

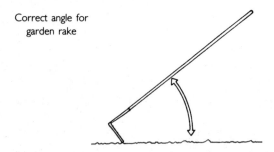

Correct angle for garden rake

★**Trowel** This is used for all planting up to the size of hole requiring the effort of a spade. An essential hand tool. Also useful for digging out larger weeds, including deep-rooted weeds in lawns.

Tools for Cutting

Saw Beginners are unlikely to need a saw unless they have inherited with their first garden an ancient, decrepit or diseased tree that needs help or is beyond it. In such an event it is better to invite someone with more knowledge and experience to tackle the work.

Secateurs need skilful use and a beginner with a new, rough plot is unlikely to have a use for them initially. Eventually they may become part of the general furniture that travels round the garden in your pocket. Do not be tempted to buy a cheap pair. There are two basic designs:

Anvil: The cutting blade cuts against a flat blade. The best anvil secateurs are pivoted in such a way that the blade pulls back as it cuts, thus avoiding crushing the stem.

Bypass: The cutting blade passes the bottom arm.

Uses:

● Pruning and removing dead heads of flowers

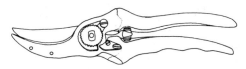

Bypass secateurs

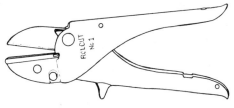

Anvil secateurs

★**Shears** You may not need these in your first year but it will not be long before you find a use for them.

Uses:

● Trimming hedges

● Cutting long grass

● Cutting down green manures before incorporating into the soil (see p.40)

● Pruning certain shrubs, such as heathers and *Potentilla* species

● Cutting down old stems of herbaceous plants in autumn or spring and similar work in summer

Scythe or **Hook** Born-again rustics and old hands love the long-handled, two-handed, traditional scythe. Few people actually know how to wield it efficiently and effortlessly. The small one-handed grass hook is more useful and simple to use. It works even better used in conjunction with a crooked stick in the other hand.

Uses:

- Cutting long grass
- Clearing tall weeds on neglected plots
- Cutting down green manures before incorporating into the soil (see p.40)

Tools for the Lawn

★**Edging shears** are simple long-handled scissors for trimming grass along lawn edges. If you have a lawn, these are essential.

Edging shears

Edging tool ("half-moon" edger) The semi-circular blade of this simple tool is designed purely for cutting turf. Use it for making neat edges to beds and for cutting turf when laying a lawn.

Edging tool

14

Lawn rake This differs in shape and use from the garden rake. The head is usually fan-shaped and the teeth longer and thinner or flat, bent at the tips for collecting up material. Those with stiffly sprung wire teeth are often referred to as "spring tine" rakes.

Uses:

- Raking up grass mowings and long grass
- Raking up leaves
- Scratching moss from lawns
- Scarifying lawns (see p. 75)

Lawn rake

Some Other Useful Equipment

- Canes of different lengths
- Sufficient hosepipe to reach all of the garden from your tap, with connectors
- Measuring stick, marked to make it easier for you to plant out at correct spacings. (A yard or metre in length is a good size.)
- Netting for protecting crops (with wire hoops)
- Two pegs and a length of string to make a line
- Pocket knife
- Plant labels
- Sprayer
- String
- Water butt to collect water from a shed or garage roof
- Watering can with a fine rose
- Wheelbarrow

Chapter 2
SOIL

To A GARDENER soil is not 'dirt'. Despite its rather lifeless and immobile appearance it is, in fact, on the move constantly — if not visibly. Soils have been created by millennia of geological and climatic activity to reach a stage when they can support life. If you scoop up some earth from a healthy garden you will be holding in your palm, along with the rock dust and fragments of decaying vegetation, a busy community of billions of microscopic organisms and fungi.

You may also have noticed that soils can differ in appearance. The colour gives some clue to the kind of soil that you have. Clays tend to be yellow, red or grey; silts, peats and sands come in darker shades; chalky soils are usually rather pale with obvious lumps of chalky stone. But there are other secrets to be revealed which will give you a better indication of your garden's "bank balance".

Topsoil and Subsoil

If you dig a hole or trench on your plot, you will find that the appearance and texture of the soil alters considerably as you go down. It is, in fact, divided into identifiable layers which should never be mixed. The topmost layer (*topsoil*) is the active layer, supplying most of a plant's growing needs. Here, in a healthy soil, organisms large and small abound. If you are lucky, you may have 30 cm (12 in) or more of topsoil before reaching the *subsoil*, which may be of clay, sand or stony. It is hard to describe the transition from topsoil to subsoil, but it will be obvious that you have reached a separate layer because the appearance and structure of the soil will be different.

Subsoil contains some plant foods but is generally not fertile and supports little life, apart from the occasional nomadic worm. Deep-rooting plants such as trees and shrubs and even some vegetables can make use of these buried nutrients.

Finally you will reach the rock layer from which your soil was originally created.

Soil Types

Topsoils vary according to the different particle types they contain. These particle types are listed below.

Clay Clay particles are very small indeed and flat in shape. They stick to each other with the same tenacity as two sheets of wet glass, causing the soil to drain badly. Without careful management, clay particles can coagulate and bake to an impenetrable solidity or, at the other extreme, add several surplus pounds of gunge to the soles of your boots. Clay is, however, full of plant food, which it releases under friendly management. Clay soils are usually yellow or grey and are cold soils, warming only slowly in spring. You will, therefore, need to sow seeds rather later in spring than you would with other soil types and the growing season may end rather abruptly when cold weather arrives in autumn.

Silt has many of the disadvantages of clay without its inherent fertility. The particles are slightly larger than clay but still heavy to work. Silt may be dark brown or grey in colour and has a distinctly smooth, silky feel to it. The particles pack together very tightly and thus drain poorly.

Sand The largest particles in the soil, apart from stones and pebbles, are sand. Any visit to a beach will show you how sand allows water to drain rapidly and starts to dry out with the first hint of sunshine. Few plants can grow in pure sand, but sand mixed with other particles helps to make soils better drained and friendlier to plant roots and gardeners' tempers. Sandy soils are warmer than clays, and so seeds germinate more quickly, giving a few extra valuable weeks to the growing season. Pure sand contains no nutrients, therefore you can expect a sandy soil to need feeding (see chapter 4).

Peat In a few parts of England the very slow decomposition of mosses or sedges in wet conditions has led to the formation of a dense black soil called peat. Peat soils have little plant food and tend to be extremely acid (see below).

Humus When plants and animals die, the remains rot down and become part of the soil again. Careful inspection of a good soil should reveal these rotted and semi-rotted remains, usually dark or brown and crumbly. This organic matter, which good gardeners supply in large quantities (see p.32) to their plots, is high in plant foods and the basis of soil fertility. It has beneficial effects on all soil types: it improves drainage in heavy soils but acts as a sponge to soak up excess water; it darkens pale soils; it opens up silts and clays, but gives body to light sands.

Chalk Chalk soils are amongst the most difficult to manage. The topsoil is often not very deep, full of stones, strongly alkaline (see below) and, even worse, sitting over solid rock. Some plants, however, will flourish even in these conditions.

Loam is a description of combinations of the above particles with the dominant one giving the soil its name (i.e. clay loam, sandy loam etc.). Occasionally but rarely a soil may consist of only one type of particle. This is true particularly of peat soils.

Soil Acidity

Soils are described as *acid* or *alkaline*, depending on the amount of calcium-supplying lime that is present. Just as some humans have adapted to living in extreme conditions, so too have some plants — but generally garden plants, especially food crops, prefer conditions that are neither too acid nor too alkaline.

Acid soils have little lime. They release their nutrients quite readily, which can be a problem if no plants are actively growing to make use of them. In high rainfall areas this can mean that plant foods are lost by leaching, often into nearby rivers and water courses to cause the now familiar ecological damage. Earthworms need calcium and so tend to shun acid soils. Micro-organisms, too, find it hard to survive very acid conditions. Peat soils (see p.18) were created by just these factors and can remain in a relatively stable semi-rotted state for centuries.

Lime, ideally in the form of ground limestone or dolomite, can be added to acid soils to make them less acid (see below).

Alkaline soils may have quite high levels of lime. Calcium, the principal constituent of lime, makes strong chemical bonds with the minerals that feed plants. This can be useful since leaching is therefore less likely but also a nuisance if the effect is to prevent the plant getting its food. Earthworms thrive in these soils and soil life is generally more active, counteracting to some extent the action of the calcium. Some ornamental plants such as heathers, rhododendrons and others (see the lists on pp.145-52) will not tolerate alkaline conditions.

Alkaline soils should never be limed. It is possible to make acid soils more alkaline but the reverse is extremely difficult. Manure, lawnmowings and soil preparations made from composted shredded bark or woodchips will have a small effect over a period of regular use.

Applying Lime

The most commonly available form of lime is hydrated lime, often simply labelled 'garden lime'. Organic gardeners use ground limestone or dolomite in preference as these are less soluble and their effects last longer. Dolomite is a ground rock containing calcium and magnesium, another important plant food. Calcified seaweed is also suitable and has the added benefit of containing a fairly full range of trace elements (see p.31).

The amount of lime needed to raise the pH of a soil is given below and will vary depending on the type of soil.

To raise the pH of a soil by 0.5, apply:-

Light sandy soils – 250 g/m^2 (8oz/sq. yd)

Medium loams – 550 g/m^2 (1 lb/sq. yd)

Heavy clays – 800 g/m^2 (1½ lb/sq. yd)

Notes:

1. Never lime alkaline soils.

2. There is no inflexible natural law about the timing of lime applications. It makes sense to scatter it when rain will take it down and when the soil is relatively unimpeded by crops and plants.

3. Deeply entrenched tradition claims that lime and manure should not be applied together. In fact, if the manure is well worked in to the soil and is dark and rotted the possibility of nitrogen (see p.30) being lost as ammonia gas does not occur. There is no adverse chemical reaction between lime and compost.

Taking Tests

A fairly reliable assessment of the lime content of your soil can be done with a simple kit available in any garden centre and is well worth doing. The acid/alkaline balance is referred to as the pH with a number ranging from 0 to 14. The central figure of 7 indicates a neutral soil that is neither acid nor alkaline. Most soils will range from 4.5 (very acid) to 8.5 (very alkaline) and these conditions need different treatment (see p.19). If your soil is neutral-to-acid, you can grow most ornamental plants with ease.

The pH should be checked every third or fourth year on fruit and vegetable plots (or once a year on a quarter of the plot), but you should be careful not to lime plots where potatoes are likely to be grown within two years (see *Crop Rotation*, p.45). Unlike most other vegetables, potatoes can tolerate fairly acid conditions. You should aim to achieve a pH of about 6.5 to 7.0.

Several laboratories offer a soil test service to reveal not only the pH of the soil but also its nutrient content. These services are advertised in most gardening magazines. Home testing kits are not really accurate enough to be of much value. However, such test results need to be treated with caution: in warm weather soil activity is greater and more nutrients will be present. Moreover, organic gardeners increase the nutrient content of their soil by using compost, manure and other organic matter which release nutrients slowly and steadily (see pp. 32-45), and these "invisible assets" will not be revealed by an on-the-spot "statement of account". A service more suited to organic gardeners is provided by the Elm Farm Research Centre (see p. 156 for address). The report form may look alarmingly scientific but the section on plant foods later in this book (see p. 31) should help you understand the script.

Soil Inhabitants

Some of the soil inhabitants are very easily spotted. Most people recognize earthworms which, since Darwin revealed their importance, have acquired if not a cuddly image, then at least a high level of respect. Worms ingest soil, extract from it what they want and expel as wormcasts a substance miraculously many times richer than the original soil. They also, by tunnelling, create networks of passages which, if left undisturbed, provide routes for air and water as well as draining the soil. Many other creatures live in the soil: snails, slugs, millipedes, centipedes, beetles, woodlice and larvae of a host of insects. Most of them are busy feeding on decaying plant matter (and thereby improving the soil) or on each other and can be tolerated and, in many cases, encouraged. The chart on p. 118 gives more information. In time they will all die and add to the soil humus.

Equally important but less obvious are the hordes of microscopic bacteria and fungi which live entirely on the decaying humus in the soil. By breaking down the original plant material they release the simple minerals which plants need to grow, thus completing a neat cycle. (See chapter 4 for more information on the nutrients plants require.) These micro-organisms (which number greater in a teaspoonful than all the human population of planet Earth) need a regular supply of organic matter in order to survive. Chemical fertilizers are about as much use to their metabolism as a can full of lurid E numbers is to us – they may even subdue their activity.

What Kind of Soil is Yours?

There are two simple ways of finding this out:

THE MODELLING TEST

a) Pick up a handful of damp but not saturated soil.

b) Squeeze some between finger and thumb:
> Gritty — sand
> Smooth and silky — silt
> Sticky — clay

c) Roll it into a sausage and then try to form a ring:
> It falls apart readily — sand
> It makes a sausage but not a ring — silt
> It can be easily modelled and holds its shape — clay

THE SEDIMENTATION TEST

a) Find a narrow bottle or large test tube.

b) Quarter fill it with a representative sample of your soil, removing any large stones or bits of plant debris.

c) Top up to three-quarters with water and shake the bottle vigorously until all the soil has dissolved. After one hour shake it again.

d) Leave it for 24 hours. The particles will have settled into clearly visible layers: sand on the bottom, followed by silt, then clay. Any humus will probably be floating. The relative size of the bands will tell you your soil type.

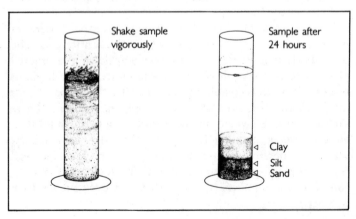

Shake sample vigorously

Sample after 24 hours

Clay

Silt

Sand

Chapter 3
GETTING THE
BEST FROM
YOUR SOIL

Y OUR SOIL IS your greatest asset. It pays to feed and manage it well — the result will be bigger crops, better flowers, lusher lawns. Soils do not change their basic nature: a clay loam cannot become a silt and vice versa. However, all soils can be improved with good management. We talk about "feeding" soil partly because it is the living organisms in the soil which contribute to its structure and these organisms need food. Their favourite food, of which they never tire, is organic matter, i.e. compost, manure and other plant debris. Organic matter makes humus which has several beneficial properties:

- It retains water and releases it slowly to plant roots.
- It binds soil particles into clumps (known as "crumbs"), thus aiding drainage and making it easier for roots to penetrate.
- It is attractive to earthworms and their beneficial effects (see p.21).
- It lightens heavy clays and silts and gives body to sandy soils.
- It darkens light-coloured soils, helping them to warm up more quickly and retain heat longer.
- It activates soil micro-organisms, which break it down gradually, releasing plant foods as plants need them.

You should not get the impression from this that every inch of your garden needs to be knee-deep in muck. Organic matter can be supplied in many forms, details of which are given below. The section *Feeding Your Plants* (see p.31) gives an approximate guide to rates of application and should be read in conjunction with this one.

23

Other substances can be used to improve the structure of clay soils:

Dolomite and ground limestone are not only of use to raise the pH (see p.19). They also help acid clay soils to break up into granular crumbs by a process known as "flocculation". Lime used for this purpose is usually applied in autumn, scattered on the surface (see p.19 for rates of application). Not all clay soils are acid, however, and if you have an alkaline clay you will have to rely on organic matter or gypsum.

Gypsum is the main ingredient of the plaster used by builders. It is chemically different from limestone but applied at 125g/m^2 (4 oz/yd^2) has a similar flocculating effect. Gypsum can be used on alkaline clay because it does not raise the pH.

Coarse grit and sharp sand are sometimes used on heavy clay to open up the structure by purely physical means. Builders' sand is not suitable as it is too round and smooth to have the desired effect.

Seaweed meal is dried, ground seaweed more usually used as an organic fertilizer (see p.41) for the potassium it has collected from our rich oceans. The sticky alginates seem to help to break up solid clay lumps into finer crumbs. Seaweed meal should be worked under the surface in autumn or in late summer before a green manure (see p.37). Left on top it turns to a slimy gel.

Drainage

No matter how well you feed your soil, if it drains badly few plants will prosper. With the exception of plants that colonize wet and waterside areas, most plants cannot tolerate prolonged waterlogging and I have yet to see an English rice paddy.

There are a number of possible causes for poor drainage, some natural and some man-made. The first time that you become aware of a problem will be when you notice that, after heavy rain, water does not drain away but remains in puddles or boggy areas. The problem may be at the surface, especially on lawns, or much deeper.

HIGH WATER TABLE

There is a level in all soils below which the earth is saturated. This level (the water table) varies according to locality but will be higher in winter than in summer.

To cure No amount of digging will deal with this. If you plan to grow fruit or vegetables, you will have to lay artificial drains to take the water away. Alternatively, you could live with nature and grow plants that enjoy these conditions.

POOR SOIL STRUCTURE

This is a frequent problem in gardens of new houses after the builders have left. The passage of large vehicles or piling of heavy building materials crushes the soil particles together and prevents water from percolating through the soil.

To cure Organic matter is probably already beginning to sound like a panacea. Where poor structure of the soil is the problem, as it might well be on a badly managed clay or silt, the addition of compost and manure will indeed make a noticeable difference. If the problem persists, however, other measures, such as deep digging or drainage pipes, may be necessary.

SURFACE COMPACTION

This is most common on lawns — especially if the FA Cup is regularly re-enacted there when the ground is wet or if a regular pathway is created to, for example, a garden gate or the compost heap. It may also be a problem on vegetable plots which have been walked on regularly, especially during wet weather. In these instances the problem is usually only at the surface.

To cure Compacted lawns can usually be easily cured by spiking the surface (see p.75). Digging will break any surface compaction on vegetable plots but where there has been severe compaction you may have to dig quite deeply.

NATURAL HARD LAYERS

These are sometimes created by the presence of high levels of aluminium, iron and some other minerals in the soil. You may discover this when digging as a solid barrier, although it is often deeper than the penetration of a spade or fork.

To cure On a vegetable plot or new flower bed this can best be cured by hand digging to whatever depth is necessary to break the impermeable layer. On lawns the simplest cure is to break the pan every 30 cm (12 in) or so by driving an iron spike through it with a sledge hammer.

N.B. Rotovators can also cause problems with drainage. Whilst it is an excellent tool for breaking ground and creating a fine surface for seed-sowing, a rotovator can, if used regularly on the same plot as the only means of turning the soil, create a smooth, polished "pan" at the level reached by the blades. This polished layer will need to be broken by digging.

Laying Drains

Draining land involves a great deal of unavoidable hard work. There are several methods of laying drains. This is the one I consider to be the simplest and most convenient.

STAGE 1
Unless aided by a pump, water can only run downhill. If there is no convenient ditch or stream at a low point in your garden into which to drain the run-off, you will have to create a soakaway (see diagram).

STAGE 2
If you have sloping land running down to your garden, you will have to cut off any seepage that would rapidly fill up your

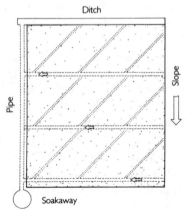

carefully drained soil by digging a ditch across the slope above
the area which you are draining. This ditch should be 90 cm
(3 ft) deep and be connected to the run-off point or soakaway
by another ditch.

Plan of drainage system

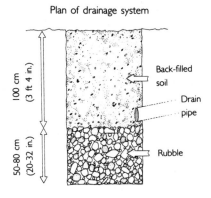

STAGE 3

The hard work continues with the laying of the main drainage
system.

Materials required:

- Pea gravel or small rubble
- Drainage pipes — available as rigid or flexible perforated plastic or short sections of earthenware land
  drain

You will need to plan for a main pipeline into which other
pipes will run at an angle. This may be in a herringbone
arrangement or into one side only with the main pipe
discharging eventually into the ditch or soakaway (see diagram).

Each run should be separated from the next by 12 m (40 ft)
for sandy soil, 9 m (30 ft) for medium loams and 4.5 m (15 ft)
for clay.

Trenches should be at least 60 cm (2 ft) deep, and you
should remember to keep topsoil and subsoil separate, with a
slight fall of 1 in 40 to the main pipe. Spread 5 cm (2 in) of

gravel on the bottom of the trench, lay the pipe and fill the trench with gravel or rubble until the pipe is no longer visible. Pipe junctions should be covered by a slate or tile to prevent soil blocking the hole. Replace some of the subsoil and all the topsoil. The remaining subsoil will have to be removed.

More ingenious and adventurous gardeners could harness this waterflow to create streams and ponds. This is not a project for beginners.

Digging and Not Digging

Digging is described as single or double, depending on the depth of soil disturbance. Single digging involves turning over the top spade's depth of soil, whilst double digging is intended to loosen soil to two spade-depths. Digging methods are covered in chapter 5 on pp. 57-8.

REASONS FOR DIGGING

- Curing drainage problems.
- Burying weeds (see p.126).
- Incorporating compost or manure.
- Creating new beds or vegetable plots.
- Exposing clay soils to weathering. Frost breaks solid clods of heavy soils and, in combination with other remedies (see above), helps create that finely crumbled surface needed for sowing.
- Some pests lay eggs in the soil or overwinter as cocoons below the surface. Digging throws these into the open where beady-eyed birds pick them up with relish.

The first simple observation to make about digging is that it is either hard work or very hard work, depending on your fitness and state of health. So is it really necessary? Some gardeners love the sound of metal on soil, the shining sod, the rhythmic exercise. A well-turned plot can sit as neat and smug as well-turned phrases on a writer's page — but the poetry is all in the eye. For earthworms and soil-living creatures digging is an invasion of their order, destroying burrows and turning their world upside down. Let me assure you that on many soils it is possible to garden without doing much digging although, as we have already seen (*Drainage*, p.24), digging does have benefits and uses.

At the National Centre for Organic Gardening we have a demonstration "no-dig" plot laid out in the standard fashion, which maintains an excellent soil structure despite being walked on during gardening operations. Our soil is a sandy loam; it is unlikely that a clay soil would be so obliging. At the Northern Horticultural Society gardens in Harrogate the soil is an unfriendly clay. Here they have experimented successfully with narrow beds which become more and more workable as the years pass with minimal digging and no gardener's boots tramping over them.

REASONS FOR NOT DIGGING

- The natural structure of the soil is retained and soil organisms are not disturbed.
- Weed seeds can lie dormant but still viable below the surface for forty years or more. Digging brings them into the light and air where they rapidly germinate.
- Organic matter remains mostly within the top few centimetres of soil, creating a steadily improving surface structure. Soil activity is most lively in the top 15 cm (6 in).
- Less physical effort is required.
- Digging over silt, sandy or peat soils in autumn or winter has no beneficial effects. In fact such soils are likely to slump and compact under snow and winter rain.

(For further details of growing without digging see p.83.)

Chapter 4
GROWING PLANTS

What Do Plants Need?

W ATER, AIR AND SUNLIGHT: these three elements make up the survival kit for plants, allowing them to gather energy from the sun, remain erect and draw plant food from the soil. It is these plant foods that give the plant its health, vigour, flowers and fruits. Any plant can survive with low levels of plant food but will not grow much, may show strange colourings and easily succumb to pests and diseases. The plant foods are divided, not by importance (for all are important) but according to the quantity of each demanded by plants, into three groups: major nutrients, minor nutrients, trace elements.

MAJOR NUTRIENTS

Nitrogen is recognized as the most important of all. This element is essential for the growth of stems and leaves and gives a plant its vigour. It is represented in scientific and gardening literature and on bags of fertilizer by the letter N.

Phosphorus, sometimes also referred to as phosphate and represented by the letter P, is essential for the growth of roots and shoot tips and so is often applied prior to planting trees and shrubs. Sandy soils can occasionally be low in this mineral.

Potash, or more correctly potassium (K), plays a major role in plant health and contributes towards flowering and fruiting. The balance between nitrogen and potash is important as it enables plants to combine adequate healthy growth with a good show of flowers or fruit. Sandy soils can also be low in potash.

Bags of fertilizer (even organic ones) will show levels of the major nutrients (N:P:K) as a ratio. Some fertilizers play a specific role (see below) but general-purpose fertilizers should have roughly equal proportions of these nutrients. The percentages of these nutrients will not be high: typically less than five per cent of each.

MINOR NUTRIENTS

Needed in smaller quantities but nevertheless important to plants are calcium (Ca), magnesium (Mg) and sulphur (Na). All of these have one or more specific functions in the healthy growth of plants.

TRACE ELEMENTS

Only minute quantities of these (a 'trace', hence the name) are required. Trace elements include minerals such as copper, iron, boron, manganese and zinc, each of which performs a vital role in plant metabolism. The shortage or excess of one of these can cause quite remarkable results. For example, insufficient molybdenum in a soil can cause cauliflowers to produce tail-like leaves that have only midribs, a condition known as "whiptail"; more commonly, on alkaline soils raspberries develop very yellow young leaves, showing insufficient iron is available. Sometimes, as in this case, the shortage may be induced by the pH of the soil (see p.20). Except in these instances, organically managed soils are rarely deficient in trace elements and cope with excesses by holding minerals in reserve in the organic matter content.

Feeding Your Plants

We have already seen how important organic matter in the form of compost, manure and other plant material is to soil structure. Now we find that these magic substances also feed plants. This should be no surprise, since the nutrients originally gathered by plants are simply being returned for re-use. The rate of release of these nutrients is determined by the activity of soil organisms, which work faster at higher soil temperatures as long as there is enough moisture and air present. Below of about 6°C (42°F) there is little activity.

31

Plants are not gluttons and prefer their food in a regular, steady supply rather than all at once. The ubiquitously quoted "4 ounces per square yard" of instant chemical powders takes no account of this, whereas nature, being rather clever, has organized things so that soil organism activity more or less matches plant food demands. Organic matter supplies the raw material for these soil organisms and also improves soil structure. Chemical fertilizers do not affect structure, nor do they feed soil organisms — they may even depress their activity. Chemical fertilizers are intended to feed plants directly with an instant "shot". The role of organic fertilizers is described on p.40. Organic matter comes in several forms:

COMPOSTS

Compost is the product of rotted garden waste. It is still actively decomposing, slowly releasing its nutrient content. The plant food value of compost will vary according to the ingredients, but, in theory at least, it should be of perfectly balanced composition and will certainly contain the trace elements. All gardeners should make compost (see p.48 for details of how to make it). It is part of the recycling process that allows life on earth to continue.

Mushroom compost can be a valuable soil conditioner with plenty of plant foods left after the mushrooms have had their share. Mushroom compost is the rotted horse manure discarded by the mushroom industry at the end of the process. Organically produced mushrooms are rare, so most mushroom compost on sale is likely to contain the pesticides used to control pests and diseases. It also contains lime and so is not suitable for alkaline soils or lime-hating plants.

Worm compost is fun to produce, especially if you can develop a warm and loving relationship with the striped brandling worms which will turn your kitchen waste into concentrated goodness. Details of making worm compost are on p.53. The end product is so rich that it is best used as a fertilizer spread by the handful and is perfect added judiciously to potting soil where plants are going to grow in pots with a restricted root run. It is also useful sprinkled on the soil surface to revive and feed tired house plants.

MANURE

Manure is a combination of animal droppings and, usually, straw. The most commonly available nowadays is probably horse manure, not, as once, from the hard-working predecessors of the motor engine but from horses whose only work is the pleasure of humans. The manure is just as good but quite often horses are stabled nowadays on sawdust or wood shavings. This takes much longer to decompose and should not be used until it is well rotted, which may take a year. Mature horse manure is ready for use when it is dark and the original ingredients are barely discernible.

Cow manure is usually referred to as farmyard manure for obvious reasons. Some farms, however, sell pig or poultry manure. These may well be the emptyings of intensive livestock units or battery henhouses. Apart from the possibility of hormones or antibiotics finding their way through the animals' digestive tracts, there may be moral implications here for you to consider. Increasingly, poultry and pigs are being kept in more humane conditions and there is no need to turn up your nose at manure from these farms.

Poultry manure and pigeon manure are both very strongly ammoniac — an indication that they have high levels of nitrogen. This can scorch plants, so the manure is best used as an ingredient in the compost heap (see p.50).

It is best to buy your manure unrotted during the spring or summer when the barns are being emptied. Cover it with a plastic sheet weighted at the edges. This sheet will prevent rain washing out valuable plant food and retain heat and moisture during the rapid decomposition that will take place. The end result should be dark brown and very moist with just traces of the original straw.

Manure under
polythene

APPLYING MANURE AND COMPOST

Manure and compost can be applied at any time. The most convenient times usually turn out to be late summer/autumn and spring. Some crops, especially vegetables, have a greater need than others but, as a general guide, one barrowload should be enough to cover 4m^2 (4 yd^2). Compost can safely be applied at twice this rate.

The list below gives typical instances when you might apply manure and compost:

- As preparation for the potato plot (see *Crop Rotation*, p.45).
- When making a new shrub or flower bed or fruit plot.
- As a mulch for roses or fruit (use compost rather than manure for strawberries).

Large amounts of manure are not necessarily needed on every inch of the garden. It is possible to overfeed plants, especially if you are using fertilizers as well. This is more of a danger with instant chemical fertilizers than with the slow-release organic ones. Curiously, plants can show deficiency symptoms when there is too much of a plant food present. It is not uncommon for non-organic gardeners to produce toxic levels of potassium and phosphate in their soils through overuse of chemicals and then be mystified at the failure of such pampered plants. The *Crop Rotation* section on p.45 gives you a manuring programme for your vegetable plot.

LEAFMOULD

Every autumn billions of leaves part company with their parent tree and fall to the ground. Many gardeners still regard these as a nuisance. As a result all over the country dense, choking smoke rises from smouldering piles of leaves and council refuse tips are the only beneficiaries of those collected from urban streets.

Leaves are, however, an important and valuable resource. Rotting leaves release their plant foods very slowly. This slow breakdown makes them ideal for conditioning soil (see p.23). They are particularly useful in creating fine seedbeds (see p.107) and, in this respect, are excellent for clay soils. Spread them on the surface in the autumn where carrots or parsnips are to be sown or anywhere where you are making a seedbed.

Leaves also make a good mulch material (see below) on flower beds and shrub borders. Here they help to structure the soil without adding too much plant food, which might make plants excessively bushy and leafy and less generous in flowering.

Wherever peat might be used in the garden, it is worth substituting leafmould. Peat is sold as a substance for improving soil structure, as a surface mulch (see below), or for use in home-made potting mixtures (see p.63). Two million tons of peat are extracted every year in the UK for the garden trade alone. The peat bogs are conservation sites of international importance as well as being stable repositories of large amounts of carbon. Extracted peat releases its carbon to add to the assault on the ozone layer.

ORGANIC MULCHES
Mulching describes the process of laying material over the soil surface. This material could be plastic or peanut shells but for the purpose of this chapter we are dealing with methods of feeding soil and plants and so are interested in organic mulches. The benefits are many:

- Weeds are suppressed.
- Water is retained.
- Soil activity is encouraged at the surface.
- The soil surface is protected from heavy rain.
- Warmth can be retained in the soil if the mulch is applied to warm soil.
- Plant foods are slowly made available.
- Mulches such as straw can be used to keep mud from splashing onto low-growing fruits such as strawberries and bush tomatoes.

Listed below are materials suitable for mulching, showing their particular values. A mulch is not a dainty light sprinkling but a good thick layer 3—5 cm (1—2 in) thick. It is also intended to remain on the surface, decomposing slowly, rather than be forked into the soil. Many of the substances listed are only partially or not at all rotted and would actually reduce

Mulches should always be laid onto soil that is warm and already moist.

Manure will feed soil and plants. It is ideal for mulching roses and fruit trees or bushes, but is not a weed suppressor.

Compost has similar properties to manure. It could also be used round shrubs which need a boost.

Leafmould is an excellent soil conditioner. Use it on shrub borders, flower beds, herbs. It is a moderately good weed suppressor but occasionally contains weed seeds.

Hay makes a dense weed-suppressing mat. It is good for "no-dig" potatoes (see p.84), round fruit trees and bushes, and for conserving moisture round courgettes and marrows.

Straw has similar properties to hay but is not so long-lasting. It is good weed suppressor but sometimes still contains grain seeds. Inorganically-grown straw will contain residues of pesticide and weedkiller. Organically-grown straw is useful round strawberries, bush tomatoes and anywhere where hay might be used. It is also used to make paths between vegetable beds.

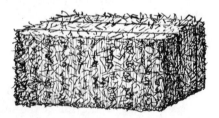

Straw

Newspaper makes an even more effective weedkiller than hay or straw alone. Spread out at least six pages thick, overlapping at the edges and covered with hay or straw, it will kill out some of the more persistent weeds (see p.128). Newsprint no longer contains large quantities of lead and will not poison soil. It is particularly useful between rows of raspberries or round bushes or trees planted in weedy or newly created beds.

Lawnmowings will provide some plant food and conserve moisture over short periods. They tend to rot quite quickly. Large quantities of lawnmowings can sometimes be an embarrassment. Mulching makes use of such gluts.

Wood chippings

Ornamental bark mulches, composted wood chips are now readily available from garden centres. They are not cheap but will last two or three years. Their best use is as long-term weed control on beds of ornamental flowering plants, shrubs and trees that have been cleared of all difficult weeds (see p.128). Not suitable for use in vegetable or fruit plots.

Shredded prunings are a cheaper alternative to ornamental mulches. If allowed to weather for a year they take on a less glaring colour but they can be used immediately.

GREEN MANURES

A green manure is not a pile of green dung but a leafy crop grown specifically for the sake of the soil. There are a number of plant types ideally suited to this purpose, some used more commonly than others. The crop is sown, allowed to reach a lush but immature stage and then either dug in or killed with a light-excluding mulch such as black polythene, old carpets, newspaper or a thick application of hay or straw. The dying plant remains are too young to have tough stems and so rot quickly, activating soil organisms and fulfilling all the functions of a manure.

Green manuring is cheap and simple. For the cost of a packet of seeds (for sowing rates see chart) you gain a great many benefits:

- Green manures protect soil. Bare soil, particularly if left over winter, can be battered and compacted by heavy rain and snow. The leaves of the green manure break the fall of the raindrops whilst the roots protect the soil structure.

37

- Some green manures germinate and grow very quickly. These can be used to keep the soil in trim during a gap between crops.

- The pea family have a relationship with certain organisms which make nodules (tiny knobbly growths) on their roots. As part of the deal these organisms "fix" nitrogen from the air. A number of green manures belong to this family and thus, when dug in, give you a net increase in nitrogen. Other green manures have very long roots which reach deep into the subsoil, collecting nutrients from parts that other plants cannot reach. These become available in the topsoil when the plant is dug in.

- Other types can be used to hold on to the valuable plant foods already there so that you do not lose them. It takes longer, for example, for the soil to cool in autumn than for the air. As a result the soil organisms are still actively making plant food available. If there are no plants present, as is often the case in autumn, the first heavy rain will wash many of these nutrients beyond the reach of future crops.

- Green manures produce dense, swamping growth that gives little room for weeds.

SOME SIMPLE USES FOR GREEN MANURES
To protect soil over winter

Suitable crop	sowing details	sowing rate	notes
Grazing rye	broadcast in September or early October	$32g/m^2$ ($1oz/yd^2$)	Dig in during March or when flower head can be felt in the crown. Can also be sown any time from March.
Tares	in drills or broadcast late July/early August	$10g/m^2$ ($1oz/4yd^2$)	Fixes nitrogen. Dig in during March or when first flowers show. Can also be sown in spring.

For short-term use between crops

Mustard	broadcast any time from early March to late August	25g/5m^2 (1oz/6yd^2)	Can be dug in after 4-8 weeks.
Phacelia	broadcast any time from early March to late August	25g/3.5m^2 (1oz/4yd^2)	If left to flower will attract bees; can be dug in after 4-8 weeks.
Fenugreek	broadcast May to early August	25g/5m^2 (10z/6yd^2)	Culinary spice. Fixes nitrogen. Can be dug in after 8-10 weeks.

For long-term use

Essex red clover	broadcast any time between April and late July	25g/8m^2 (1oz/10yd^2)	Popular with bees and beneficial insects (see p.118). Can be dug in at any time, once it has formed a good soil cover.
Alfalfa	broadcast any time from March to August	15g/m^2 (½oz/yd^2)	Fixes nitrogen if the correct bacteria, available in powder form, are added to the soil. Without the bacteria, alfalfa makes a lush, weed-suppressing growth with extensive root systems. Can be dug in at any time, once it has formed a good soil cover.

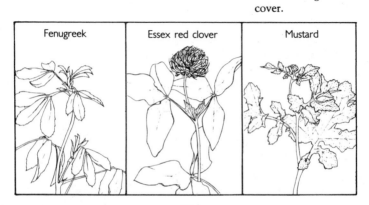

Fenugreek | Essex red clover | Mustard

39

USING GREEN MANURES

Seeds are either broadcast or drilled (for an explanation of these terms and details of sowing see pp.60-62) according to their size. They can be sown at any time between early March and mid-November depending on their use and hardiness. Ideally green manures should be dug in before they flower but, if the ground is needed sooner, there is no need to wait. It is best to dig in the manure crop about two to three weeks before you plant out seedlings or shrubs. Sometimes seeds sown immediately after a green manure has been dug in germinate poorly.

The chart on pp.38-40 shows which green manures suit specific uses and gives details of sowing rates and times.

Note: If your green manure is left a little too long and becomes tough-stemmed, cut it down with a scythe or rotary mower set for a high cut and compost the tops. The roots can then be dug in.

Green manure plants, in most cases, belong to families that include common vegetables. They should, therefore, be used in accordance with the principles of crop rotation (see p.45).

Some crops used as green manures are suitable for long-term use and these can be allowed to flower freely. Two typical examples of this use are given below.

Example 1: You plan a shrub border or flower bed but feel that the soil is not very healthy. Perhaps you are, in any case, saving up to buy the plants. The bed can be dug, sown with a green manure and left for a year. The green manure is dug in before planting the bed.

Example 2: You take over an established garden and find a bed of rather tired and spindly roses. The soil obviously needs a rest and can be sown with a green manure after removing the roses and manuring the land, whilst you decide what to do with it next.

FERTILITY IN A BAG – ORGANIC FERTILIZERS

There are some die-hard traditionalists who believe that nothing will grow without four ounces per square yard of something out of a bag. Was it by some miracle that generations of cottage gardeners grew bountiful crops without these products? If you feed your soil well you will find that plants do not miss their spring-time bag of sweets. There are instances, however, where extra fertility may be needed. Some soils are naturally short of certain plant foods or are so alkaline that they are reluctant to release them. You may have taken over a garden which has been badly managed, with a soil that is starved and lifeless. Small gardens do not easily accommodate a set of compost bins or a pile of manure. These are among a number of instances where additional fertility may need to be or is more conveniently brought in by the bag. The most useful organic bagged composts and fertilizers are listed below, with a description of their use. It should be remembered, however, that these products do not have the bulk of compost, manure and green manure and, therefore, do not supply on their own the valuable humus needed by soils. They should always be seen as sources of additional or complementary fertility, a side dish to the main course of manure or green manure. A small garden, for example, could be managed using either bagged organic concentrated manure or fertilizers — *and* green manuring.

Concentrated manures are used as general-purpose fertilizers. They are derived from a variety of animal manures or composted materials, including wormcasts or duck manure. Some of them, particularly those produced from poultry manure, may be the product of intensive livestock systems and, therefore, of morally questionable origins. These latter products may also contain unacceptable levels of hormones or chemicals. The Soil Association symbol gives a guarantee of organic authenticity to any bagged manure which displays it.

Seaweed meal is a dried, crushed seaweed product rich in the trace elements and with a good level of potassium as well as some nitrogen. It is useful for flowering and fruiting plants growing in soils that are short of potash and also for balancing plant food where too much nitrogen is available. Seaweed meal also helps to condition clay (see p.24). Apply it in the autumn and mix it into the top few inches of soil.

Calcified seaweed is a crushed, coral-like substance suitable for supplying calcium and magnesium or correcting trace

41

element deficiencies. Its structure makes it a good soil conditioner. It can be used instead of lime (see p.19).

Liquid seaweed, used as a foliar spray, appears to have a beneficial effect on plant health and growth. No one quite knows why, since its nutrient content is very low. However, plant food enters the metabolism of a plant more quickly through the leaves and it is possible that the trace elements present may improve the transfer of nutrients within the plant. Liquid seaweed is useful for correcting trace element deficiencies during the growing season.

Bonemeal is high in phosphates. Use it scattered lightly into planting holes for trees and shrubs to improve rooting and therefore establishment of the plant.

Blood, fish and bone sounds rather grisly but has been the basic general-purpose fertilizer in gardens for decades. The potash level is not high but there is plenty of nitrogen and phosphate. Mixed with seaweed meal in equal quantities, it makes a general-purpose feed for plants that are regularly heavily pruned or are showing signs of poor growth (but see *Note,* below). Also use it as a lawn feed in April (see p.77).

Hoof and horn is a good source of slowly released nitrogen. Use it in spring, if necessary, round plants that are regularly heavily pruned, such as raspberries and blackcurrants.

Ground limestone is used to correct the pH (see p.19) and supply calcium.

Ground dolomite is another pulverized natural rock product, which supplies long-lasting calcium and magnesium. It is also used to raise the pH (see p.19).

Rock phosphate is a natural rock mined for its use as a slow-release source of phosphate. Use it on soils that show a deficiency in your initial soil test report (see p.20).

Rock potash is another ground rock containing potassium. Its potash is very slowly released and it is doubtful if it would have a major effect on a well-managed soil. Research is continuing in order to establish its true value.

Note: Deficiencies are very hard to diagnose accurately, particularly for beginners. If a plant is not growing well, you should check to see what else might be the cause before assuming that deficiency is the problem. Deficiencies in a well-fed soil are rare. Here is a checklist to help you:

- Are other plants nearby showing similar symptoms?
- Does the plant have enough water?
- Is it too heavily shaded?
- Are there signs of serious pest or disease attack?
- Is the pH high? Some plant foods become progressively less available as the pH rises above 7.0.
- Is the temperature suddenly colder than normal? Sometimes in spring plants try to grow faster than can be matched by the availability of plant foods, especially if a warm spell is followed by a cold one. Plants recover happily from this.
- Could the symptoms have been caused by frost or wind?
- Has it had too much fertilizer? See p.34.

RUSSIAN COMFREY

Russian comfrey is a plant that well earns its keep in an organic garden. Its long taproot fetches potash from deep in the soil, concentrating it in large leaves. The leaves have little fibre and rot quickly. An established clump can be cut four or five times in a year and the leaves used as a mulch (see p.35)

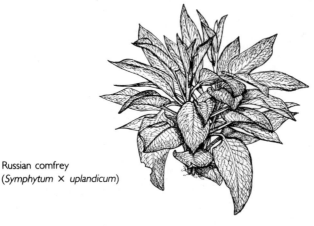

Russian comfrey
(*Symphytum × uplandicum*)

round tomatoes, buried in a trench before planting potatoes or harvested to make a liquid feed (see below).

Russian comfrey can be bought either as potted plants or as pieces of root, each of which will produce a new clump. Plant them in well-manured soil between April and September 60 cm (2 ft) apart. Keep them weeded and watered. Once established they will not need watering but give them an annual mulch of strawy manure or compost, if you can spare it.

Comfrey should be cut just before flowering and allowed to wilt before use unless you are going to put it into a liquid concentrate barrel (see p.45). Sometimes, if not wilted, cut leaves root to form a new plant, generally somewhere really inconvenient. Stop cutting comfrey in September and allow the last flush of foliage to die down on the plant during winter.

LIQUID FEEDING

Liquid feeding is a method of supplying a regular small dose of diluted plant food in a form that plants can use immediately. This practice goes against the usual organic principle of feeding the soil rather than the plant. However, where you are growing plants to maturity in a limited space such as a "growbag", plant pot or other container, you will have to feed them eventually as they will soon run out of food.

You can buy organic liquid feeds, based usually on seaweed or manure, but you can also make your own very simply.

Manure Tea Not the sort of thing to invite the vicar to enjoy. Suspend a small bag of manure in a barrel of water and leave it to steep. Use about a 10-litre (2-gallon) bucketful of manure to 114 litres (25 gallons) of water. After two weeks you can start using it undiluted. You can continue to tap manure tea from this right through the season. Discard the manure in the autumn on to the compost heap.

Nettle knockout Cut young nettles in the spring and stuff them into a barrel (preferably one fitted with a tap). Fill the barrel with water so that you have about 5 litres (1 gallon) of water to each ½ kg (1 lb) of nettles. After two to three weeks it will be ready for use. Dilute the fermented liquid in 10 times the volume of water. This turns plants lush and green and humans weak-kneed and green – the aroma is very organic!

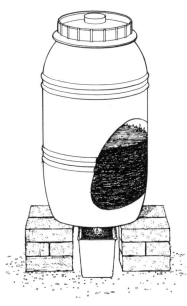

Comfrey barrel

Comfrey Concentrate Drill a hole in the bottom of a barrel and stand it high enough off the ground to fit a container underneath (see diagram). Cut your comfrey before it flowers and fill the barrel to the top with dry leaves, pressing them down firmly. Cover with a lid and leave to ferment without water. After three weeks or so a black liquid will start to drop into the container. Dilute this with 15 or 20 parts by volume of water before using it. This concentrate is comparable to any of the commercial brands of chemical liquid feed.

Note: The size of container used for these preparations can easily be adjusted to suit your needs.

USING LIQUID FEEDS

Outdoor crops generally do not need feeding. If you have a greenhouse, however, plants growing in the border soil can be fed up to twice a week in mid-summer, whilst any hanging baskets, tubs, growbags or pot-grown plants should be treated three times a week at the dilution rates mentioned above. You can feed less frequently early and late in the season when plant growth is generally slower.

Crop Rotation

If you grow a particular type of vegetable in the same spot in the garden year after year, this venue becomes in time a popular locale for all the pests and diseases common to that plant. In addition the soil may eventually become depleted in

45

one of several plant foods for which that crop has a special hunger. The solution to this is a system almost as old as farming called "crop rotation".

In this system, vegetables are grouped according to their botanical family into three or four convenient groups to match three or four plots in your vegetable garden. This gives rise to the expression "three-course" or "four-course rotation". The whole group is moved onto another plot each year so that no family of plants grows in the same soil for two consecutive years (see diagram). Some of the green manures also belong to these families and should be fitted in to the rotation accordingly.

You may be tempted to grow a lot of one particular crop because you especially like it or eat a lot of it. You will have to adjust your appetite, however, to ensure that the crop fits within the rotation. It would be fine, for example, to fill one whole quarter or course of the rotation with potatoes but more than that would not work on a four-course system.

SOME COMMON VEGETABLE FAMILIES

Potato family	**Pea family**	**Cabbage family**
potato	all peas	Brussels sprouts
tomato	broad beans	cabbage
	french beans	broccoli and calabrese
	runner beans	cauliflower
		kale
	Green Manures:	radish
	alfalfa	swede
	Essex red clover	turnip
	fenugreek	
	tares	**Green Manure:**
		mustard

Spinach family	**Marrow family**	**Onion family**	**Carrot family**
spinach	marrow	onions	carrot
swiss chard	cucumber	garlic	parsley
beetroot	courgette	leeks	parsnip
	pumpkin	shallots	

Note: Lettuce belong to the daisy family. Because they are fast-maturing, they are usually fitted in between crops or in odd gaps where space allows. Ideally they too should be rotated.

The following rotation plan is only a suggestion. If you decide to grow fewer crops you could use a three-course rotation. Any combination of family groups is possible if it works for your system. The important point is that plants within a family are always kept together. It is also more convenient if plants with similar soil treatment requirements occupy the same plots.

YEAR 1

	(Before planting: Test pH and add lime if needed—see p.19)		(Before planting: Manure if not done in autumn)	
B	Pea family Onion family followed by tares or grazing rye		Potato family Marrow family followed by grazing rye	A
	Cabbage family		Carrot family Spinach family Sweetcorn	
C	(Mulch in summer with lawn mowings or compost)		(After cropping: Manure and green manure any vacant ground, if possible, before potatoes are planted)	D

YEAR 2

C	B
D	A

YEAR 3

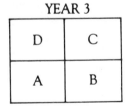

D	C
A	B

YEAR 4

A	D
B	C

Chapter 5
GARDEN WORK: BASIC TECHNIQUES

Making Compost

COMPOSTING IS NOT an art form. Whilst its action on soil may seem magical, its preparation carries no mystique. It is a straightforward, practical operation that enables you to recycle most of the plant foods in your garden to be used time and time again in the endless cycle of fertility.

Any pile of plant debris will rot down eventually but, by employing certain practices and principles, we can speed the process and improve the end result. The compost heap is a bacteria and fungi farm and consequently it is subject to the laws of nature. These various organisms operate at different temperatures and at different stages of the decomposition process. Initially the heap should become very hot, typically at least 60°C (140°F), as a result of which weed seeds and disease spores are killed. As it cools different organisms set to work on the tougher material; and finally earthworms and larger creatures move in to finish the job. Ideally a heap should be maintained at about 45°C (113°F) but this is hard for gardeners to achieve.

In the depths of winter few creatures are active and little decomposition takes place, whereas in the higher temperatures of summer the whole process can be over in six weeks. The following sections take you through the composting process one stage at a time.

STAGE 1: BUILDING A BIN
Compost bins can be bought from garden centres, but you do not need to be a cabinet maker to build your own. Your bin should have:

Solid sides These help to prevent the outside layer from drying out and improve insulation so that less heat is lost. Wood is a better insulator than plastic. Wire mesh is not suitable on its own but makes a very cheap alternative if lined with old carpet or cardboard.

Surface cover The damp, rotting compost produces a great deal of heat and steam. A piece of old carpet or hessian will keep in the heat while allowing some moisture to escape.

Protective lid A non-porous lid will keep out heavy rain, which can cool the heap, and prevent drying out caused by sun and wind.

Removable front Don't forget that you will eventually need to get at the contents. The front can be a simple board or a more sophisticated system of sliding planks (see diagram).

The ideal size for a compost bin is 1 m^3 (approx. 1 yd^3) i.e. 1 m (1 yd) high, wide and deep. Smaller containers will work but they tend to lose heat more rapidly unless you can find a cunning way of insulating them.

Ideally, you should have a second bin for turning the heap (see p.52).

Construction method for New Zealand compost box

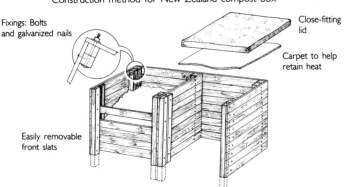

Fixings: Bolts and galvanized nails

Close-fitting lid

Carpet to help retain heat

Easily removable front slats

STAGE 2: SITING THE BIN

Although the compost bin is the heart of the organic garden, it does not need to take pride of place.

- It can be tucked away tidily behind a hedge or screen but should not be in deep shade

49

- Cold, windy sites should be avoided
- If the bin is erected over soil it will greatly ease the passage of earthworms and other creatures into the contents
- Allow room for manouevring barrows

If your bin is easy to dismantle and reassemble it could be moved to a new site each year.

STAGE 3: FILLING THE BIN

What comes out of a heap is determined by what goes in. There is plenty of margin for error in the equation but what you should try to achieve is a balance between tougher materials such as dead plant stalks and soft, fibreless ingredients such as lawnmowings. Grass clippings are useful to get the rotting process started (see *Activators*, below) but, if mixed in too generously, will make a fetid, slimy heap. Tough stalks on their own will decompose very slowly. The chart below gives a list of suitable materials for composting and shows their relative "toughness" or "softness".

Compost ingredients
This is not a complete list: it is intended merely as a guide.

Tough	Medium	Soft
Cabbage stumps	Potato haulms	Lawn mowings
Old weed stems	Young prunings	Kitchen scraps
Straw	Long grass	Young weeds
Newspaper	Hay	Young nettles
Sawdust★	Old houseplants	Seaweed
Wood shavings★	Hair	Pigeon manure
Winter prunings	Strawy manure	Poultry droppings

★ It is best to keep these to small quantities only as they are particularly tough.

NB: Leaves from the autumn fall are best rotted on their own as the decomposition process is slightly different and they have a special value (see *Making Leafmould*, p.56).

There are other important factors to ensure good composting:

- Place a layer of cabbage stems, twigs or prunings at the base of the heap before you start filling. This aids drainage.

- Avoid filling a bin a bit at a time. If you cannot fill at least half the bin at one session, then save up your ingredients in bags or in an empty bin until you have enough.

- Chop up or shred (see p. 52) any large leaves, stalks or whole plants.

- Load the bin in layers of at least 15 cm (6 in), mixing the ingredients well as you go.

- Ensure that all the contents are thoroughly wet without being swamped. Watering each layer with a hose or watering can will achieve this better than trying to do it *after* the heap is built.

- Dogs, rats and foxes will all be interested in your heap if it contains cooked food or meat scraps — avoid these.

- Use at least one material that will start the rotting process quickly (see *Activators*, below).

- Some gardeners like to add lime to their heaps. This is not necessary.

- Large amounts of soil should not be added to the heap. The few crumbs clinging to the roots of weeds are quite enough to supply the "starter kit" of composting organisms.

- Cover the heap with a carpet and a lid.

Activators are so called because they start the process of decomposition with a flourish of heat and steam. Nitrogen is required in the breakdown process and these materials have plenty of it readily available. Young nettles and lawnmowings in moderate quantities are both excellent for this purpose, as is animal or human urine. Poultry and pigeon manure are too rich to use on their own in the garden but make excellent activators. There are a number of proprietary preparations of activator available but these tend to be preparations of chemical nitrogen with the exception of two types: herbal activators and cultures of selected composting bacteria and fungi in powder form.

Shredders The more surface area available for composting organisms to process, the faster a heap decomposes. Some plant leaves and stalks can easily be chopped with shears or a spade, but a mechanical shredder allows you to compost cabbage stems, prunings, small branches and other rather unyielding garden waste, thus making bonfires even more unnecessary (see p.80). Shredders powered by electricity are useful and relatively cheap but not as powerful or effective as the larger petrol-driven machines.

STAGE 4: TURNING THE HEAP
After two or three weeks of decomposition the contents will have slumped and the temperature of the heap will have dropped to ambient air temperature. You do not need a thermometer to test this — a probing digit or plunging hand for the less squeamish will suffice. The next stage is not essential but, since most of us do not build perfect heaps, it will help to improve the final product.

By "turning the heap" we mean either forking it out of one bin and into another or removing it and putting it back. This stirs air into the heap which generates more energy for a second heating and cooling session. At this stage you also have the chance to add more water if your heap is too dry or to adjust any imbalance between soft and tough materials by adding the relevant ingredient (see the chart on p.50 for details).

Compost tumblers You are almost certain to come across these in your local garden centre. They are designed to stir air into the contents by regular daily turning, involving no forking but actually some effort as the contents progressively shrink and alter the centre of gravity. The contents stay hot for longer in these but will need to be turned out to mature once they have cooled. These tumblers are useful for speeding up the compost-making process and for dealing with smaller quantities of compost.

COMPOST TRENCHES

In winter little decomposition takes place and large amounts of kitchen waste can accumulate before you are ready to make a new heap. One way of dealing with this embarrassment is to bury the waste in the ground. Normally this would not be a good idea as nitrogen needed to break down the waste would be borrowed from surrounding soil. Any plant grown on this plot would therefore be deprived of nitrogen until the kitchen waste had rotted.

Runner beans, however, obtain their nitrogen from the air and will not miss it if it's in short supply in the soil. In any case they are planted quite late in the season and so the compost should have rotted quite a lot by then. Runner bean compost trenches are therefore a very good way of dealing with winter kitchen waste.

Method Mark out the rows where your runner beans will grow. Dig a trench to the full depth and width of the spade along the line of one row. This can be gradually filled with kitchen waste until it is full to the top. If your soil is acid (see p.18), scatter some lime or calcified seaweed into the trench as it fills. Cover the trench with the heap of soil and dig out the next trench. You can bury cabbage stumps in this way too, although it is advisable to smash them first with a lump hammer or heavy stone. Animals can be hungry in winter and will almost certainly investigate your trench. It is, therefore, advisable not to allow bacon rind, bones or cooked food to become mixed with kitchen waste waiting to go into the trench.

Making Worm Compost

There are many methods of doing this. The one that I propose to describe is the simplest, and was devised by the late Jim Hay.

STAGE 1: PREPARING THE CONTAINER

A plastic dustbin with a lid makes an ideal simple worm bin.

Using a 6 mm drill bit, drill holes around the circumference of the bin in two rings 7.5 cm (3 in) and 15 cm (6 in) from the base (see diagram) for drainage. Make two similar rings of holes in the lid to provide air.

Now move the bin to where it is to be sited.

STAGE 2: SITING THE BIN

The worms operate best at a temperature of around 21°C (70°F), becoming progressively less active down to about 15°C (59°F). Below this temperature they are much less active and are very uncomfortable at temperatures higher than 25°C. You should, therefore, choose a site that is protected from the wind and out of direct sunlight. In the winter it is best to move the bin into a greenhouse, shed, back porch or some other protected space and wrap old carpets, bubble insulation or something similar round the bin to prevent the worms becoming too inactive or even frozen.

STAGE 3: FILLING THE BIN

Put a layer of sand and gravel in the bottom to reach a level just above the drainage holes. Soak this with water until the excess starts to run out of the holes.

Cover this layer with a wooden board drilled with holes, or a circle of old carpet or woven plastic mulch or anything that

Worm bin

6-mm holes for ventilation

Brandling worms
(Eisenia foetida)

Vegetable waste stuffed down between bedding and wall of bin
75 mm bedding
Perforated board

175 mm sump
(2 parts aggregate, 1 part sand)

will serve to keep the drainage material separate from the compost.

Put in a 7.5-cm (3-in) layer of bedding. This can be sawdust, old compost, leafmould or peat (ideally the less acid sedge peat). Any of these could be bulked out with shredded newspaper. It should be thoroughly moist but squeezed out to ensure that it is not waterlogged.

STAGE 4: THE WORMS
The large pink earthworms that are turned up in digging are not composting worms. The right creature for this job is smaller, ringed with darker bands and usually found in old manure heaps, compost and under leafmould. You may find you already have some but, if not, fishing tackle suppliers often sell them as bait under the name "brandling worms" or they can be obtained by mail order. To make a good start you will need 100 or so worms — more would be better. To give the worms a chance to establish themselves it is best to start them off in spring or early summer.

Place the worms in the bedding, add no more than a few handfuls of "food" (see below) and cover the whole thing with damp sacking or newspaper.

STAGE 5: FEEDING THE WORMS
These worms will feed on anything that is decaying but their best use is as a means of processing kitchen waste. Add no more than a 10-litre (2-gallon) bucketful at a time and wait until the waste is well populated and breaking down before adding the next batch. Tuck the food down one side to allow the worms to colonize it at leisure or retreat if it heats up (as it may well in summer). Ensure the contents are never too wet or too dry. Large lumps and cabbage leaves should be chopped up. Worms do not like very acid conditions. It is a good idea at least once in the period of filling the bin to stir in a handful of lime or calcified seaweed. You should not be alarmed to find tiny thread-like white worms in the bin. These are doing the same job as the brandling worms but can tolerate more acid conditions. Worms can survive without feeding for some time and you will not need to put them into kennels whilst you take your annual holiday.

STAGE 6: EMPTYING AND USING THE CONTENTS

When the bin is almost full or you want to use the compost, add one last layer over the surface and allow the worms to colonize it.

Scoop this off with the top 75–100 mm (3–4 in) of dark composted waste and set it on one side to start the next bin.

Worm compost is not produced in huge bulk but is very rich.

Use it to:
- Make potting composts (see p.63)
- Feed garden plants
- Feed house plants in pots
- Mulch

Making Leafmould

If leaves are left where they fall they play the important part in conservation that they have always played, being food or home to many creatures, including hibernating hedgehogs. On the other hand leaves can be collected and stacked in loose heaps to rot slowly. A simple wire enclosure will prevent them from blowing away.

The rotting of leaves is principally a fungal process, slower and cooler than composting. The leaves need only to be wetted thoroughly if they are dry. Without any further additions the leaves will decompose in two years. If space is limited this can be speeded up in one of three ways.

Lawnmowings can be mixed into the leaves in the spring following their collection at the rate of 4 parts leaves to 1 part mowings by bulk.

Diluted urine (with 4 times the volume of water) can be watered onto the pile as it is built and subsequently throughout the year as it becomes available.

A rotary mower run over the leaves before collecting them up will shred the leaves finely and mix in some grass clippings. Alternatively, feed the leaves through a shredder before stacking.

All these processes will give you leafmould in one year.

Digging

Digging is a strenuous activity. It can be good for you and it could be crippling. There will be occasions when you will need to dig. There will also be those gardeners whose relentless attraction to the well-turned sod may convince you that digging is an essential part of good garden routine.

The section on *Digging and Not Digging* (p.28) should help to give you a more balanced view as well as explaining the terms.

GENERAL TECHNIQUE

- Use a spade that suits you in length and size.
- Don't take on more than you can comfortably manage at one session, particularly with double digging.
- Keep a straight back and a straight spade.
- Don't try to turn too large a piece of soil at a time.

SINGLE DIGGING

1. Dig a 30-cm (12-in) trench across one end of the plot and barrow the soil from it to the far end.

2. Turn the next 30 cm (12 in) into this trench, working systematically across the face. Ensure that weeds are buried.

3. Continue to work backwards until you have an empty trench which you then fill from the pile of soil originally removed.

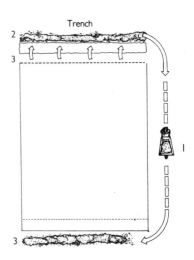

Notes:

1. Manure can be worked into the soil as you dig.
2. Do not expect to have a perfect clear 30-cm (12-in) trench all the way through the operation. It will not work out like that in practice.

DOUBLE DIGGING

1. Mark out a strip 60 cm (2 ft) wide across the plot. Strip off any turf and pile it at the far end.

2. Dig out the topsoil, scooping up all the crumbs, and barrow it to the far end.

3. Break up the subsoil with a fork *without turning it.*

Trench

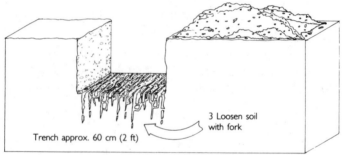

Trench approx. 60 cm (2 ft)

3 Loosen soil with fork

4. Move your line back 60 cm (2 ft), strip off the turf and drop it into the empty trench.

5. Pile the topsoil on top, scoop out all the crumbs as in 2 and then break up the subsoil as in 3.

6. Continue working backwards until you can fill in the last trench using the stacked turf and soil.

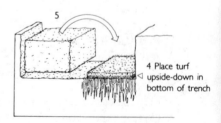

4 Place turf upside-down in bottom of trench

Sowing

Buying young vegetable or flower seedlings for transplanting from a garden centre or by mail order can help to ease the beginner into a more gentle start. There is, however, always just a chance that these seedlings may harbour one of the more unpleasant intractable diseases or pests. It is also unlikely that they will have been raised organically, although, no doubt, as the years go by it will become easier to find organic transplants.

Sowing seeds cannot be avoided, however, if you plan to grow a reasonable range of vegetables. Tomatoes, cucumbers, lettuces, courgettes, runner beans, cabbages and Brussels sprouts are all readily available as seedlings but carrots, beetroot, parsnips and peas amongst many others are not. Growing from seed also gives you a wider selection of varieties and types as well as the opportunity to give your plants the full uncompromising organic treatment from the start.

SEEDS

A seed is a storehouse of energy waiting for the right conditions to burst into growth. The more vigorously and robustly a plant begins its life, the better chance it has of surviving to maturity. Seeds lose their potential rapidly in the wrong conditions. To prevent this happening it is best to store even newly bought packets in a dark, cool and dry place, preferably in an airtight jar (kilner jars are ideal).

Many seeds nowadays are treated with chemicals prior to packing. Organic gardeners can avoid these by buying from HDRA, Chase, Suffolk Herbs or those companies that offer a range of untreated seeds in their catalogues (see p.157).

Some seeds have a remarkably long shelf life if stored well, but no seed lasts forever and some, such as parsnips, have a very limited life indeed. It is not worth keeping these for the following year — the results will be very disappointing. If you have some old seeds and you are not sure if they are still viable, sow some on a piece of wet tissue and see how many germinate. Gardeners seldom, if ever, keep seed in optimum conditions. As a rough guide, I would suggest the following maximum storage dates:

One season only	Up to 2 years	Up to 3 years	Up to 4 years
Parsnip	Onion	Lettuce	Tomato
	Leek	Cauliflower	Radish
	Runner beans	Cabbage	Courgette
	French beans	Brussel	Marrow
	Broad beans	sprouts	Cucumber
	Parsley	Broccoli	Pumpkin
	Spinach	Turnip	Beetroot
	Carrot	Swede	Chard
	Most flower	Peas	
	seeds		

SOWING OUTSIDE

In nature, all seeds are sown on the ground where they fall. The simplest way to start plants in the garden is to sow them outside either directly where they are to grow or in a specially prepared seedbed. If you confine yourself to this method alone you can still grow quite a respectable list of flowers and vegetables but a greenhouse or warm windowsill offer you broader and more adventurous horizons (see *Sowing Indoors*, p. 62).

For most crops, gardening books and seed packets will tell you to sow in a drill. This is a shallow furrow in the soil made with the edge of a rake or draw hoe. The depth will depend on the size of the seed, varying from 5 cm (2 in) for peas and beans to 5 mm (¼ in) for lettuce, carrots and other small seeds.

1. Rake the soil to a smooth surface.
2. Peg out a line where the seeds are to be sown. Draw the edge of a hoe, rake or similar V-shaped tool along the line to leave a shallow depression.

3. Sow the seed in a single thin row in the furrow with no clumps. Larger seeds should be spaced about 2.5 cm (1 in) apart. Alternatively sow pinches of 5 or 6 seeds at intervals along the row to match the eventual spacing — which will be stated on the packet.

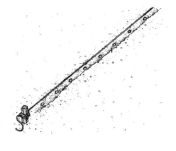

4. Cover the seed by pulling the back of the rake along the top of the drill and tamp it down firmly.

5. Mark the row with a label, showing the variety and date of sowing.

Note: If the soil is dry, you should pour a line of water into the drill *before* sowing the seed. Water sprinkled on the surface quickly evaporates.

Thinning In nearly all cases you will sow more seed than you need. When the plants are just 5 cm (2 in) or so tall, they will need to be thinned by pulling out surplus seedlings. The back of the seed packet will tell you how far apart to leave the selected seedlings. Spring onions and radishes do not need thinning. Peas and beans are large enough to sow individual seeds where you want them to grow.

Broadcasting is a seed-sowing method, not a description of a proud allotment holder's harangue. Seed is scattered on the surface and raked in to grow unthinned where it germinates. This method is suitable for most green manures, grass and certain salad crops such as cress and salad rocket, which are harvested as seedlings.

SOWING INDOORS

Some of our most popular vegetables and a great many favourite flowers can only be successfully grown if given an artificially extended season by starting them off indoors when it is still cold and damp outside. Even for a number of those plants which could be started outside, there is a distinct advantage in sowing them indoors where conditions during the delicate early weeks of their life can be better monitored and controlled.

You do not need a greenhouse for indoor sowing but it helps a lot. I use the bathroom, others use a kitchen windowsill. The results are adequate but not as good as in a greenhouse where the all-round light prevents plants from becoming stretched and leggy as they reach towards the window.

SEED AND POTTING COMPOSTS

It is confusing that the mixture in which seeds are sown is also called "compost". Seed and potting composts, however, are very different from garden compost. It is possible in these more enlightened days to buy quite a range of organic potting mixes. There are several types:

Seed compost has a low nutrient level. Seeds sown in this will need to be moved to a richer medium once they have produced two or three true leaves. (The first leaves to appear are seed leaves, which are simpler in shape.)

Potting compost has a richer food supply and is used in the next stage of growth up to the time that the plant is ready for transplanting (see p.68).

General-purpose compost (which, to add to the confusion, is often also referred to as "potting compost") is the only kind a beginner really needs. It is suitable for raising plants from seed to transplant stage without any pricking out (see p.68).

Use it for any flowers or vegetables which can be transplanted such as cabbages, tomatoes, lettuces, courgettes, sweetcorn and beans.

Note: Beans have enough food supplies in the seed to grow to transplanting size without a rich compost. A mixture of 50:50 good garden soil and leafmould both shaken through a large-mesh soil sieve will be cheaper and perfectly adequate.

Home-made compost If you are planning to grow any plants in large pots or tubs, it becomes expensive to rely on bought-in potting mixtures to fill these containers. Because of the confined space, soil alone will not provide enough food for the restricted roots. The following formula is a good and cheap home-made mixture:

4 × 10-litre (2-gallon) buckets of your best garden soil

2 × 10-litre (2-gallon) buckets of leafmould (or peat)

1 × 10-litre (2-gallon) bucket of worm compost, well-rotted manure or garden compost

125 g (4 oz) bonemeal

250 g (8 oz) seaweed meal

60 g (2 oz) calcified seaweed, ground limestone or dolomite

Note: Plants grown in pots or containers will need liquid feeds (see p.44).

SOME COMMON TERMS EXPLAINED:

Plants are described as *annual, biennial* or *perennial.* Any of these might be prefixed by "*hardy*" or "*half-hardy*".

Annual The lifecycle of the plant is completed within one year. Many popular flowers, as well as the majority of vegetables, fall into this category.

Biennial Plants in this group live for two years. In the first year growth is concentrated into producing leaves and roots. Flowering takes place in the second year. This group includes wallflowers, sweet Williams, Canterbury bells and many root vegetables, such as carrots and parsnips. These are harvested after the first vegetative phase − if left in place they would eventually flower.

Perennial plants live for several years. Some are very long-lived. The permanent occupants of flower and shrub beds will all be perennials. Rhubarb, strawberries, asparagus and globe artichokes are all perennials.

Herbaceous perennials These plants form a permanent clump or crown and foliage dies back at the end of the season. Examples include Michaelmas daisy, mint, and a number of weeds such as nettles.

Hardy plants will tolerate our climate and are not affected by frost.

Half-hardy indicates a tender disposition. These plants would be killed by the first frost of autumn and have to be grown indoors until frosts no longer threaten. Vegetables in this group include sweetcorn, tomatoes, courgettes, runner beans and potatoes (which are safe until shoots show above the surface and may regrow even if their tips get frosted).

SEEDTRAYS, MODULES AND POTS

The standard *seedtray* is a shallow, rectangular, plastic tray, either full-sized or half-size.

Suitable for:

- Pricking out (see p.66) flowers or vegetable seedlings raised in seed compost
- Sowing large quantities of seeds for later pricking out
- Sowing broad, French or runner beans (although greengrocers' discarded wooden crates are deeper and better)

Modules are a relatively new product. They are usually made of polystyrene and are constructed to make a number of regular sections or cells (see diagram). The most useful sizes have either 40 or 24 cells. It is also possible either to buy or make for yourself an insert to turn a standard seedtray into a

Polystyrene
seed module

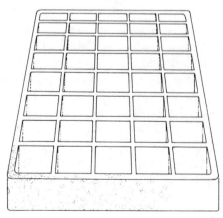

sectioned one. Because each seedling grows in its own discrete individual space, transplanting causes very little disturbance to the delicate roots. The larger 24-cell tray should be used for large-seeded plants, such as sweetcorn, that will be in the tray for some time before transplanting.

Suitable for:

- Sowing and raising most vegetables which will be transplanted
- Sowing and raising hardy annual flowers

Pots generally come into use for growing on plants that have outgrown their space (see *Potting on*, p.67). They vary in size from a tiny 5 cm (2 in) or less in diameter to over 30 cm (12 in). Pots are either clay or plastic. For the beginner plastic is preferable. The very smallest can be used for sowing individual seeds, such as sweet peas, courgettes and other large-seeded plants; the very largest are used for plants that will spend their lives in pots, usually in a greenhouse or in the house as house plants.

SOWING THE SEEDS

In pots Fill the pot to the brim with moist compost and compress lightly with the base of a pot of the same size. Make a hole in the centre about 1–1.5 cm (½–¾ in) deep with a pencil or your finger. If the seeds are quite large, sow two seeds per pot, cover with compost, and water with a can fitted with a rose. If both seeds germinate, remove one when it is large enough to tweak out. Do not overwater seeds. Waterlogged soil encourages fungal diseases. If both seeds germinate, remove one when it is large enough to tweak out.

In modules Fill the tray evenly with moist compost, compressing the contents, refilling and then pressing the surface lightly with the tool provided to leave a shallow 5-mm (¼-in) depression. Sow three or four seeds to each cell. (Eventually, you will need to thin them out to one seedling – see p.66.) Cover the seeds with compost and water gently with a can fitted with a rose.

In seedtrays Fill the tray evenly with moist compost and firm it with a board or the palm of your hand. Large seeds such as beans can be pressed into the surface in rows so that when the tray is topped up with compost the seeds lie about half-way down in depth. Finer seed is scattered thinly★ over the surface and covered with compost shaken through a kitchen sieve or rubbed between the palms of the hands. Water the seedtray with a can fitted with a rose so that the compost is wet without being waterlogged. Where only small numbers of seedlings are required, a pot could be used instead of a tray. If the seeds are very tiny it is preferable to wet the compost by standing the pots in water rather than by overhead watering. When the surface becomes dark with the absorbed moisture, the compost is wet enough and the pots can be removed.

★Sowing "thinly" is perhaps rather vague for beginners. If the seed is large enough try to ensure at least 0.5–1 cm (¼–½ in) between seeds.

Label all sowings, indicating what you have sown and where.

At this stage seeds, which are not far below or are even on the surface, must not either dry out or become saturated. If you leave a seedtray, pot of seeds or module uncovered after watering, the surface will quickly dry out. The solution is to cover the container after the initial watering until the seeds germinate. Some seeds must have light to germinate; very few need to be in darkness. Cling film works very well as a covering. The cover must be removed once the seedlings break through the surface, otherwise they press against it and try to grow round it.

Most seeds need warmth to germinate, some more so than others. Check the seed packet for the ideal temperature and try to match it as closely as you can. There is a margin of tolerance but rapid germination is preferable for most common garden plants.

PRICKING OUT

If you have sown your seeds in a pot or tray, you will soon have to give them more room to grow by pricking them out. This does not apply to beans sown in this way which can be transplanted direct into the soil. Pricking out should be done when the first two true leaves of the plant (see p.62) are clearly visible.

1. Prepare a tray of compost and make a regular series of holes (24 to a full-sized tray) with your finger or a pencil.

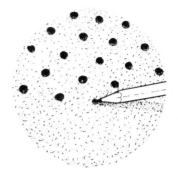

2. Hold the seedling by one of its seed leaves and, with the tip of a knife blade or a thin pointed stick, gently tease the seedling away from its neighbours.

3. Plant each seedling in one of the holes, always holding it by its seed leaf and not by its tender stem or fine roots. Firm it in gently and water the full seedtray with a can fitted with a rose.

POTTING ON

Seedlings growing in pots will eventually outgrow the space. The first sign will be roots visible through the holes in the base of the pot. To check more thoroughly place your fingers over the top of the pot so that the stem of the plant passes between the second and third finger. Turn the pot upside down and let the plant drop gently into your hand. If it is reluctant to come out tap it gently on the bottom or knock the rim on the edge of the potting bench. If the outer surface of the compost reveals a web of roots it is time to pot the plant on.

- Choose a pot not more than two sizes bigger than the original. The rootball should fit comfortably into the pot without more than a finger's width to spare all round.

- Place some compost in the bottom of the pot, drop the plant into the centre and firm compost round the sides. Tomatoes should be buried up to the lowest leaves to gain extra roots, which form along the buried stem.

- Water the pot with a can fitted with a rose to settle the compost.

TRANSPLANTING FROM SEED DRILLS

The seedlings of leeks, cabbages and others which you have sown outside will need transplanting to their growing stations once they are about 10 cm (4 in) tall.

- Unless the soil is already wet, water along the row of seedlings before uprooting them. They separate more easily with less damage to roots in wet soil.

- Choose an overcast or damp day for transplanting. On hot, sunny days plants lose much water from their leaves.

- Move the seedlings to their allotted position quickly or wrap the roots in wet newspaper if there is some delay.

- Transplanting methods and distances vary from plant to plant. Consult the seed packet or a standard gardening book for details.

- Always water seedlings after transplanting and keep them well-watered but not waterlogged until they are established.

- You can expect the transplanted seedlings to flag and wilt. Do not be alarmed. Provided that they are kept well-watered they will recover. Placing some light shading, such as old net curtain, over them will help them recover.

TRANSPLANTING FROM POTS, MODULES OR SEEDTRAYS

The process of transplanting in these instances is much the same. Plants, however, are unlikely to wilt as their roots are not disturbed. They will still need to be watered after transplanting.

Any plant sown indoors for transplanting outdoors will need time to acclimatize or "harden off" before transplanting. This is done by leaving the seedtray outside, at first by day only and then overnight as well. Careful watch of weather forecasts will be essential at this stage. This process may take up to a week.

Trees and Shrubs

On free-draining soils, trees can be planted into holes cut out just large enough to accommodate the roots easily. If you do this on a heavy soil, however, you will soon find your tree sitting in a small reservoir as all the local ground water drains into this new sump. In these circumstances you will need to cultivate an area at least twice as large as the intended planting hole before digging the hole itself to give a greater opportunity for water to drain freely. Where you are planting in an existing bed or border this should not be a problem.

CHOOSING YOUR PLANTS

- Choose trees and shrubs suited to your soil, its acidity and the site.
- Select healthy specimens with good root systems.
- Taller saplings give a greater initial impact but smaller ones are easier to maintain, establish more quickly and soon catch up.

PLANTING OUT

Shrubs are generally bought in pots, whilst trees may be pot-grown (containerized) or bare-rooted (lifted from the open ground). Roots should never be allowed to dry out. If you have received trees and shrubs by post or delivery, unpack them immediately and heel them in temporarily (see p. 71) in an unused spot if they are not in pots. When you lift them for planting out, wrap the roots in hessian or rags to keep them moist.

- Dig a planting hole large enough to receive the roots easily and about 25 cm (10 in) deep.

- Trees of more than 1.5 m (5 ft) in height will need a stake. This should be about 1.2 m (4 ft) long so that 75 cm (2½ ft) is showing above soil level after planting. Knock the stake in just off centre in the hole on the side from which the prevailing wind blows (usually SW in Britain).

- Trees and shrubs should be planted no deeper than they were previously at the nursery. A "soil mark" should be visible on the trunk. To ensure that this is done carefully place a cane or stick across the hole before dropping the tree into the centre of it: the soil mark should be level with the cane. This is especially important for trees that have been grafted (see below). If buried too deeply they will root above the graft.

- Trees that have been grown in pots should have their roots gently teased out, otherwise there is a danger

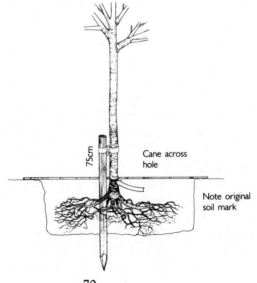

75cm

Cane across
hole

Note original
soil mark

that the roots remain restricted and tightly coiled and the tree, consequently, grows poorly.

- Scatter a handful of bonemeal onto the soil to be returned to the hole. Replace half the soil and shake the tree up and down a little to allow soil to settle between the roots.

- Checking that the tree is not planted too deeply, firm the soil gently with your heel all round, replace the rest of the soil and firm it again.

- Tie the tree to the top of the stake with a strap or tree-tie. Do not be tempted to use string. This will cut deeply into the bark and kill the tree.

- Shrubs do not usually need a stake.

Notes:

Heeling in is a term for temporary planting to ensure that roots do not dry out. Careful planting to the "soil mark" is not essential. For large numbers of trees or shrubs awaiting planting the following system can be used:

1. Dig out a trench 15—20 cm (6—8 in) deep, piling the soil on one side only. The trench should be long enough to take up to half or less of the trees and shrubs placed closely side by side.

2. Line out the first batch of plants in the trench, leaning them back against the soil heap.

3. Dig out a second trench, piling the soil onto the roots of the first row of plants. Firm the soil lightly around the roots with your heel.

4. Set out the next row and continue in this fashion until all the plants are "heeled" in.

Grafting is the process of joining two pieces of living tissue to become one. Many ornamental and nearly all fruit trees are grown on roots that were made by another tree. These roots control the size and vigour of the eventual grafted tree by giving it growth characteristics which it would not have if grown on its own roots. If soil is piled above such a graft the tree may produce its own roots and hence destroy all the benefits of grafting.

71

IN THE FIRST YEAR

The greatest threat to newly planted trees and shrubs is shortage of water. This will be exacerbated in the first season by competition from grass or weeds. The simplest solution to this is to cut a square of thick-gauge black polythene about 1 m (1 yd) square. Slit it to the centre, slip it round the trunk of the tree or shrub and anchor the edges by tucking them into the soil with the edge of a spade. If this looks unsightly to you, you can cover the polythene mat in bark mulch, wood-chips or shredded prunings. The mat can be removed after three years.

Shrubs cannot easily be treated in this way if grown in beds but should equally be kept free of weeds and well-watered in dry spells.

Looking After Lawns

The perfect weed-free striped sward has become a symbol of high-status gardening and quintessential Englishness. Lawns are frequently neglected but even more frequently are shaved and manicured to an obsessional degree. In my view lawns should meet two requirements. They should be green all year round and they should be durable enough to withstand the use to which they are put (picnics, football, croquet, pathways). To your local wildlife the perfect green sward is a dull green desert. A mixed habitat of grass species and other plants such as clover is much more interesting — and frequently more durable. Daisies, buttercups and even speedwell have great charm. You will find gardening more relaxing and pleasurable if you choose not to emulate the obsessive school. It also saves money.

MOWING

The mowing season usually starts in March and ends in October but you will not find an official "open season" date on lawns quoted in any gardeners' diary. In a mild winter, you may even find it necessary to cut the grass in early February. Assessing the correct time to start and finish mowing is a matter of careful observation.

Height of cut Many gardeners insist on cutting their lawns very short. Grasses can tolerate this up to a point, but will be considerably disadvantaged and weakened if they have little leaf growth to gather energy. Bald lawns also collect moss and weeds. The standard, general-purpose lawn contains a mixture of grass types that will be healthy and vigorous if cut *no shorter than 2.5 cm (1 in)*. Finer ornamental lawns can be cut to 1 cm (½ in).

It is important to reduce the height of the grass in stages early in the season. If you cut it down to its final summer height on the first cut you will weaken it and it will look dreadful. The first cut of the year should just tip the leaves. By May you should have progressively reduced this to the normal height for summer.

At the end of the season and during periods of drought, leave the grass longer to protect the surface.

How often? In warm wet weather grass grows very rapidly and may need cutting as often as twice a week, whilst hot dry weather or cold soil will slow growth to almost nothing. Your eye is the best judge.

Mowers The size of your lawn and the wages in your pocket will determine what sort of mower you choose. Nowadays there is an extensive choice of electric or petrol-driven models, of which the electric are generally cheaper but have the disadvantage of trailing cable across the grass — a possible hazard and limitation. Electric mowers must be plugged into a safety plug, designed to shut off supply if the cable is cut or faulty. Petrol-driven models can be used a long way from the house and are most suitable for those with large lawns or very long gardens.

The design of mowers varies greatly. The original old-fashioned *cylinder mower*, with blades on a rotating drum cutting against a plate, has grown up into a modern range of high-quality precision machines ideal for fine lawns. *Rotary mowers* have a propeller-type blade. Some hover, some are on wheels. These mowers are often capable of cutting quite tall, rough grass as well as finer lawns. The higher-priced models have a rear roller to produce the prized striped finish and are quite comparable in performance to a cylinder mower but usually equally expensive. If you have banked areas of grass you will need to use a two-stroke machine so that there is no danger of the lubricating oil draining to one side. A hovering mower would be ideal. *Mulching mowers* are a new breed, designed to cut the grass very finely and deposit it back on the ground to be returned to the soil (see *Using a grass-box* below). In shape they are similar to a rotary mower but the cutting chamber is closed so that grass is not discharged in lines or thick lumps but spread evenly. The cut grass disappears remarkably quickly. Manual mowers may well become more available and more efficiently geared for easier operation. If you are of normal fitness and health you should easily manage to mow a small lawn manually. Most modern petrol-powered machines will run on unleaded fuel but I find it hard to envisage catalytic convertors as standard fitments in the future.

Using a grass-box Every blade of grass removed is a loss of fertility. It is sound practice to allow the grass cuttings to be left *in situ* to add humus and return fertility. Lawns treated in this way need much less maintenance and very little feeding.

In spring, however, the early growth can be thick and lush and too dense to leave on the surface. At this time and on occasions when lawns have been allowed to grow rather long, it is best to use the grass-box or rake off the cuttings.

When choosing a mower look for one that can be used without its grass-box, even if it is fitted with one. The piles of mowings that accumulate can be used in compost making (p.48), as a mulch (p.35) or to line the trench when planting out potatoes.

STRIMMING AND EDGING

There are parts of any lawn that mowers cannot reach: edges, areas close to walls and fences, under low-growing shrubs or weeping trees, along raised paths. If these are left untended, they give an untidy look to an otherwise well-managed garden. Edging shears (see p.14) will deal with lawn edges and garden shears used for clipping hedges can deal with most other problems.

Those with less flexible knees or larger gardens may prefer to use a *strimmer*. This has a nylon line on a rotating head, which can cut into awkward corners. It can be used along fences and walls or against stone and brickwork without fear of damage but *it will harm trees and shrubs if the nylon line cuts the bark*. Small strimmers for small gardens are usually electrically powered but graduate in size and strength to two-stroke petrol-driven versions which can also be used with a rotating metal blade for tougher work such as cutting long grass or clearing neglected areas of brambles and scrub. These are known as *brush cutters* and are, as you might expect, considerably more expensive.

AUTUMN WORK

Most lawns are left unmaintained to fend for themselves. A lawn, however, needs your help just as much as the flowers and vegetables, especially if you use it for all the usual summertime activities. By the end of summer there may be compacted areas, bald patches, a build-up of dead grass stems ("thatch"), holes and divots all waiting for repair. Most lawn care is carried out in September and October at the end of the growing season.

Scarifying is the process of scratching the surface to break up the dead, fibrous layer of vegetation known as *thatch*. This can become starved of air and water. The grass will tend to root into this layer and may then suffer very quickly in dry weather. Scarifying can be done with brisk dragging motions of a spring tine lawn or a garden rake or by machine if your lawn is large. The thatch makes good compost. Thatch is less common on lawns where grass clippings are recycled and not collected in the grass-box.

Aerating may be needed over the whole lawn if your soil is heavy and drains badly. Usually, however, it is confined to those areas used frequently as paths or by amateur goal-keepers. Grass will be noticeably less vigorous in these areas and puddles may form after rain. Small areas can be treated with an ordinary garden fork. Drive it in 10 cm (4 in), rock it back and forward slightly and pull it out. Repeat this process in lines about 15 cm (6 in) apart. Motorized lawn aerators are available for sale or hire and make light work of large areas. Very heavy soils are best treated with hollow tine aerators, which remove a plug of soil and deposit it on the surface. These plugs can then be raked off.

Top dressing is rarely carried out nowadays but is possibly the most beneficial treatment that you can give your lawn. A mixture of good soil or loam, sharp sand and leafmould in varied proportions according to your soil type is raked or brushed over the surface of the lawn. Top dressing has several benefits: it improves the soil structure, levels out hollows and helps to decompose any thatch that has built up. The following formula shows the correct mixture of ingredients for your soil type:

	Parts by volume of		
	Sand	Soil/Loam	Leafmould
Light soils	1	4	2
Medium soils	2	4	1
Heavy soils	4	2	1

Notes:

i) Sand should be sharp sand and not builders' sand.

ii) Loam is the product of stacked turf, covered and allowed to rot. Good sieved garden soil could be substituted.

iii) Leafmould should be sieved. Used potting compost could be substituted or, if you absolutely have no alternative, peat.

Spread the mixture at the rate of about 1.5-2 kg/m^2 (3-4½ lb/yd^2). Work it in with the back of a rake.

Top dressing a large lawn is rather a major project. This treatment is best suited to small lawns, areas that are heavily used or perhaps areas close to the house where you want to achieve a strong visual impact of health and vigour.

Repairing bare patches Areas of bare lawn can either be reseeded or returfed. Reseeding is best done during damp weather in September; returfing can be done at any time during the winter so long as the ground is not saturated, frozen or covered in snow.

Reseeding:

1. Lightly break up the surface with a fork and rake it to a fine tilth. Add extra soil if necessary.

2. Scatter seed at the rate of 25 g/m² (¾ oz/yd²).

3. Rake it in gently and water it well if the ground is not damp.

4. Protect the area from birds, cats and humans with netting.

Returfing:

1. Cut carefully round the edge of the bare area in straight lines and remove all the soil inside to a depth of about 3 cm (1½ in).

2. Fork over the exposed area lightly, firm and rake to a level.

3. Lay new turf as described in *Laying a New Lawn*, p.104, filling any hollows with extra soil. Brush soil into the cracks.

4. Keep off the turf until it has knitted together well.

AUTUMN LEAVES

The wind has a tidy habit of sweeping fallen leaves into dense drifts. These should be raked off and piled into loose heaps to decompose (see *Leafmould*, p.34). Thinner accumulations of leaves can be shredded by the mower and left to decompose *in situ* or collected in the grass-box to rot separately for use in home-made potting mixes.

FEEDING LAWNS

If you rarely use a grass-box you will not need to feed your lawn very often. In any case, you should use organic fertilizers in response to how well (or badly) the grass has been growing during the previous year rather than as a matter of routine. The best time for feeding is in spring and not in the autumn. Strong growth in autumn makes grass prone to disease. Concentrated manures make excellent lawn food or you can use blood, fish and bone at the rate of 70 g/m² (2 oz/yd²). Liquid feeds based on seaweed or manure leave a curious, mildly lingering odour but are a fine tonic to sad lawns. Use them either in spring or early summer provided that the soil is moist.

WEEDS

Weeds are in the eye of the beholder. The fact that someone else chooses to eradicate a particular plant from the lawn need not predispose you to dislike it. The following tips should help you to control some of the common unwanted rogues.

Moss A sign of either poor drainage, poor fertility on light soil, high acidity, too much shading, too close mowing or balding raised patches on lawns. Remedying the cause will cure the problem. Rake off the moss and reseed any bare areas. Birds use moss for nest-building.

Daisies indicate high alkalinity, too close mowing or compacted soil. Daisies are hard to eradicate — but anyway rather delightful.

Clover provides food for bees and fixes its own nitrogen. It often remains green in lawns where the grass is starved and drought-stricken. It thrives in poor soil, so feeding with a high nitrogen fertilizer (hoof and horn or blood, fish and bone) or liquid feeds will encourage the grass to crowd it out.

Dandelions, docks, thistles and plantains will try to establish in any lawn. Their rosetted growth tends to smother grass and avoids the mower blades. Best cure is to dig them out with a knife or trowel. This is not as time-consuming as you might think. Dandelions make an excellent wine and a coffee substitute — the decision is yours.

Pests and diseases are not common on a well-managed organic lawn.

Pruning

Many gardeners are shy of pruning, anxious lest they cut unwisely. At the other extreme are those who attack their plants with unabashed relish, leaving a loose array of truncated sticks. Is it necessary? Trees and shrubs will certainly grow without pruning. However, centuries of gardening wisdom have brought us an understanding of how to use secateurs and shears to control shape and vigour, bring gentle order out of wilderness and improve the health of plants.

Pruning can be skilled and complex or simple. Trimming a hedge is, after all, a form of pruning. The subject is too large for the scope of this book and I would suggest that beginners consult a more specialised book before starting. I shall confine myself to covering the main principles to encourage readers that pruning is worth doing and offering some important guidelines. Many plants need no pruning and you should be clear what you are trying to achieve before you start.

WHY PRUNE?

To establish shape Early in the life of a plant pruning can help to create a basic framework, after which little work may be necessary. This kind of pruning is essential in forming well-branched fruit trees, which need regular pruning throughout their lives.

To control vigour Without regular trimming some plants would rapidly overwhelm their neighbours. On the other hand, hard pruning can generate new vigorous growth which would otherwise not occur. This latter technique is suited to blackcurrants, hybrid tea roses, buddleias and others.

To promote health Regular removal of dead or diseased tissue prevents the spread of infection. Similarly, dense growth or rubbing branches can provide conditions for fungus spores to invade.

For special decorative effects Topiarized hedges provide a good example of this. Some plants, such as the dogwoods and ornamental willows, are grown for the colour of their stems. Pruning hard encourages a thicket of young, brightly-coloured stems for the winter garden.

GENERAL GUIDELINES FOR PRUNING

- Always consult a good book before pruning a plant that is new to you. You may cut off the parts that are preparing to feast your eyes with flowers.

- Always use clean, sharp good-quality tools. Dirty, blunt secateurs spread disease and damage stems.

- Never leave a stub of wood with no point of growth at

the top. Cut back to either a branch, a healthy shoot or a bud.

- When removing a branch do not cut into the raised collar next to the main branch or trunk. This collar will form the tissue that seals the wound after cutting.

- Large branches should be removed in sections so that the weight of the branch does not tear a strip of bark and wood away from the cut. A shallow cut underneath the branch will also help to prevent this.

- When pruning to a bud, choose a bud pointing in the direction that you want. Prune at an angle sloping with the bud without cutting too deeply behind it (see diagram).

- Prunings of healthy wood can be shredded and composted. Diseased material should be burnt.

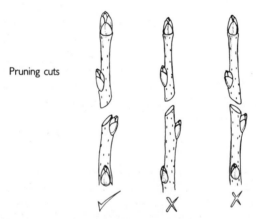

Pruning cuts

Bonfires

Gardeners who indulge their pyromania with a regular choking fire of weeds and leaves are more than just a nuisance. Bonfires waste nutrients and break the cycle that allows plant foods to be almost infinitely recycled. The smoke is also many times more carcinogenic than cigarette smoke. Organic gardeners prefer to make compost heaps and leafmould to produce substances that feed soil and plants without waste.

Weeds, leaves and prunings burn down to an ash that is composed largely of calcium (lime), baked soil particles, some phosphate, salt and varying amounts of very soluble potash. Any nitrogen present originally is lost. Fires are nature's chemical factories but the end product poses as many potential hazards to the local ecology as some factory fertilizers. Because the ingredients of the ash are very soluble they are quickly dissolved and washed away, especially on light, sandy soils, taking with them other important trace elements. Those gardeners who regularly use bonfire or wood ash as a garden fertilizer may actually be reducing the fertility of their soil, especially if the ash is applied to the same area of ground in successive years. The salt contained in the ash is poisonous to plants and soil organisms and can turn clay soils into an unworkable glue.

Not all garden waste can be recycled through the compost heap. If you have no access to a shredder, thick prunings and broken branches will have to be burnt along with all diseased and virus-infected material. Compost heaps that heat well will kill many disease organisms but not all of them. Soil-borne disease, in particular, can be quite tenacious. A bonfire means certain death.

The least toxic bonfire burns hot and fast with little smoke. To achieve this:

- Allow prunings to lose their sap and greenness before burning them.

- If possible keep the ingredients dry or wait for a period of sunny weather to dry out the wood.

- Build the fire up slowly with paper and kindling rather than stuffing a few sheets of paper into the middle of a stack.

- Lay branches or limbs across the flames in one direction. A criss-cross net of branches can create a bridge and the fire may burn out underneath.

- Keep the fire attended to ensure that the fire is active to the end.

- Do not put any diseased green material on until the fire is hot and flaming.

In the interests of safety:

- Piles of branches make inviting refuges for animals in winter. Build the fire elsewhere and feed material onto it from the pile or turn the pile over to check for hedgehogs and other creatures.
- Do not light fires during prolonged droughts.
- Avoid windy days.
- Always have a source of water at hand to douse the fire if it gets out of hand.
- Do not leave a fire unattended.
- Keep children and pets away.
- Ensure that the fire is burnt out before leaving it.

The ash that results can be used with caution. The safest place for it is sprinkled lightly in layers on compost heaps or scattered on the floor of a henhouse for later inclusion in the heap. Allow it to cool thoroughly without getting wet and store it in bags.

Chapter 6
SOME ALTERNATIVE GROWING SYSTEMS

Vegetables Without Digging

IT IS PERFECTLY POSSIBLE on most soils to grow vegetables without regular winter digging. The advantages of this are covered in chapter 3 on p.28. Only two or three crops need any different treatment under such a regime and they are covered below. In other respects the gardening methods are much the same except that the soil is never inverted. Organic matter is applied to the same plots of the rotation but is left on the surface rather than buried.

Green manures in a dug garden would normally be turned under. In a "no-dig" garden there are a number of options that allow the use of green manures:

- Sow a tender type (e.g. mustard or phacelia) in autumn to be killed by winter frosts. The dead haulms will protect the soil surface.

- Cut down annual green manures just at the point of flowering. Regrowth will be weak and can be hoed off and left to rot on the surface.

- Mulch out the crop with a heavy layer of wet hay, straw or with black polythene. After three weeks it should be safe to plant through this mulch.

- Pull up the crop by hand and drop it on the surface.

In all cases seedlings can be planted out as normal by raking aside the plant debris to fill the gaps between rows.

Where seeds such as carrots or parsnips are to be sown it is probably better not to precede it with a green manure but to protect the soil over winter with leafmould or polythene.

Potatoes are normally planted 15 cm (6 in) below the soil surface. To avoid digging they can be grown under a mulch:

- Spread manure over the surface at the rate of approx. one barrowload to each 2 m² (just over 2 yd²).

- Set out the potatoes at normal spacing on the surface.

- Cover the surface with a 15 cm (6 in) thick mulch of old hay. Until frosty weather is over it is best to cover this with an additional layer of polythene or old carpet to protect young shoots.

- As the shoots emerge through the mulch keep it topped up round them with grass mowings and hay or straw to ensure no light can penetrate to turn the potatoes green.

- To harvest, simply lift aside the mulch and pick the potatoes off the surface.

Note: Potatoes can also be grown under black polythene but are very prone to spring frosts in colder areas.

Runner beans enjoy cool, moist conditions at their roots and so it is normally recommended that they are planted over trenches of compost or rotted kitchen waste (see *Compost trenches*, p.53). They grow quite successfully without a trench on the no-dig system, provided that they are well mulched.

Vegetables in beds The standard way of growing vegetables is in straight rows on large plots. All gardening operations necessitate walking on the plots. The bigger your boots, the greater the damage to the soil structure. Much space is wasted in such a system in allowing room to walk between rows of growing crops.

A well-proven alternative to this is the bed system, which is growing in popularity now but is by no means a new idea. Vegetables are grown on beds 1.2 m (4 ft) wide with narrow paths between. For the most part, these paths need be no more than 30 cm (12 in) wide with wider barrow-sized paths through the centre and dividing the rotations (see diagram).

- All operations are carried out from the paths and soil is rarely trodden.

- Beds can be dug or not dug according to choice.

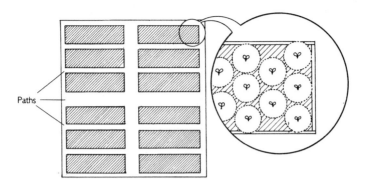

Layout of bed system showing
(inset) staggered planting method

- Soil treatments can be restricted to the growing part of the plot so that valuable compost and manure are not wasted on paths.
- Crops are set out much closer together than the standard spacing and eventually produce a dense weed-suppressing canopy of foliage.
- Because soil is not compacted, weeds are easily removed.

Vegetables are planted in blocks rather than in rows, staggered in such a way as to maximize use of space. The distance between plants is often surprisingly close since no paths are needed between rows of growing crops. If you cannot find a good book on the subject, a general guide is to plant out at the spacing normally recommended between plants in the row rather than between rows. For example, plants that might normally be planted 15 cm (6 in) apart in rows 30 cm (1 ft) apart need only 15 cm (6 in) between them on a bed.

Chapter 7
WEATHER, WIND AND WATER

※

THE BRITISH CLIMATE is not a great ally to the gardener. It may be benign in comparison with Saharan weather patterns but is wickedly fickle and frequently "unseasonal". It is no wonder that weather forecasts command such high viewing figures, especially now that they have become more detailed and accurate. The best forecasts are up-to-date local ones obtained by telephone.

Some general climatic effects can easily be predicted according to the geography of your garden. Which way does it face? How high is it above sea level? Is it low-lying compared to the surrounding landscape? How far north or south is it? Plants that fire the imagination in the catalogue may turn out to be damp squibs in your garden if you cannot offer them the conditions in which they thrive. The sections that follow should help you choose the plants best suited to your spot.

Sunshine

In the northern hemisphere the sun always travels across the southern sky. This means that gardens that slope towards the south or beds backing onto south-facing walls receive a great deal of sunlight and are consequently warmer. Gardens that are shaded from the south and open to the north receive very little direct sunshine and are cold. Similarly east-facing is colder than west-facing. The mansions of previous centuries were often laid out with careful regard for the aspect.

Modern terraced gardens, however, are rarely so well-oriented. For this reason it is important to work out how much sunshine different parts of your garden are likely to receive.

The lists on pp.147—54 suggest some plants suitable for different sites. Read the small print in your catalogues or check at the garden centre before you consign an unfamiliar plant to its possible deathbed. If you plan to grow vegetables, you will need to offer them plenty of sunshine. Most fruit also prefer sunshine but redcurrants, gooseberries and blackberries will give a crop even if they face north.

Altitude

Gardens nestling high in the hills may be several hundred feet closer to the sun but they are actually cooler and have a shorter season than nearby gardens on lower-lying land. On the other hand, low-lying gardens are much more prone to frost, especially if they are backed to the south by rising ground that does not allow frost to escape. Wind can also be an important factor in gardens at high altitudes. You can clearly see this by the way trees are stunted and pruned by the wind on mountain slopes. Establishing a garden on a windswept slope can be very difficult.

For this reason, amongst others, you should not be ruled by the calendar in your sowing and planting. The experience of neighbouring gardeners will be a valuable aid in this. Fruit and vegetables that need a long season to mature are best not attempted in gardens at high altitudes. Valley gardeners will need to take precautions to avoid losing plants to frost in spring and early autumn.

Location

Local climate varies quite considerably across Britain. It is generally true to say that the south is warmer than the north and that the west is wetter than the east. The Gulf Stream which flows up the western side of the country has some additional warming effects which allow plants common in more tropical climates to grow as far north as Scotland.

The sea generally has a buffering effect on temperature so that frosts are less frequent in coastal gardens than inland. The glens of central Scotland and the English midlands are notorious for catching out unwary gardeners with surprisingly low temperatures late in spring and early in autumn. On the other hand, coastal gardens can be lashed by furious salt-laden winds which burn the foliage of many plants.

It takes time to discover the vagaries of your local climate. There are few areas of Britain so harsh in climate that no plants will grow, but your choice of plants should be limited by an understanding of local conditions.

Wind

Wind is a regular feature of British weather. Sometimes, as we have come to know, it can be devastating in its effects. Even light winds can affect plant growth if they are persistent. These are the main effects of wind:

- Physical damage to plants.
- Reduction in temperature, therefore slower growth.
- Drying of soil causing plants to wilt.
- Distortion of plant growth caused by plants growing away from the prevailing wind in one direction. Especially noticeable in trees.
- Damage to structures such as greenhouses, frames and cloches.

WIND BARRIERS

The best defence against wind is a semi-permeable barrier that acts as a filter rather than a solid wall. When wind strikes a wall or impermeable fence at right-angles it curls back on itself at the base and passes over the top with increased force,

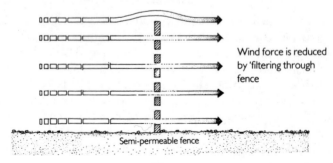

Wind force is reduced by 'filtering through fence

Semi-permeable fence

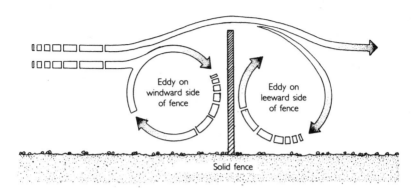

Wind accelerates over top of fence

Eddy on windward side of fence

Eddy on leeward side of fence

Solid fence

creating a similar eddy on the other side. Plants growing near the wall are pulled towards it.

Windbreaks can be in the form of hedges, groups of shrubs, fences or artificial windbreak material. The height of the barrier is as important as the permeability. The area protected is in proportion to the height: at a distance from the barrier of eight times its height, the windspeed will be reduced by half, and, at ten times the height, by only a quarter (see diagram).

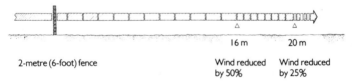

16 m 20 m

2-metre (6-foot) fence | Wind reduced by 50% | Wind reduced by 25%

Details of planting hedges and erecting fences are given in chapter 8, *Building a New Garden*.

Hedges need not be clipped. An informal grouping of shrubs of sufficient height would act very well as a windbreak. Evergreen hedges of Lawson's or Leyland cypress seem to dominate the suburban landscape. However, although they make good screens they are poor windbreaks, acting more as a solid wall than a filter. They have other disadvantages too (see *Planting a Hedge*, p.99).

The best plants for windbreak hedges are those that lose

their leaves in autumn (deciduous). Beech and hornbeam can be counted amongst these, although the dead leaves remain on the branches until new leaves form in spring. For combining conservation value with speed of growth, good windbreak value and attractive appearance, a mixed hedge of plants native to your area is ideal. A list of suitable plants is on p.152, but to achieve absolute conformity with the local flora you should check with your county conservation trust for the correct species.

Fences are hard work to erect but create a relatively instant windbreak and boundary screen. For reducing wind damage the best types are those of a more open structure which will allow some wind to pass. Alternatively you could strip alternate laths on each panel. Strong winds can tear solid fence panels from their moorings and hurl them across the garden. At Ryton Gardens we have even experienced winds strong enough to break reinforced concrete posts 10 cm (4 in) thick where solid fence panels were attached.

Windbreak netting is intended for temporary use. Most types will last for five years or more which is long enough to establish a good hedge. Windbreak netting is attached to fence posts sunk into the ground as for fencing. It is useful round fruit or vegetable plots where the posts can be permanent and the netting replaced when it deteriorates. Netting is also a good solution in windy areas where a new garden has no protection for plantings to establish.

Water

Water is an undervalued commodity. All life depends on it. Gardeners readily complain that there is either too much of it or not enough; flooding seems barely to have subsided before a hosepipe ban is in force.

Rain makes the flowers grow but when it fails we need to make the best use of the reserves kept for us by the local water company. A good gardener should know when watering is necessary and when it will be wasted. The following hints should help to show you not only how to apply water but also when it is really needed.

WATERING EQUIPMENT

Watering cans provide the main means of watering plants early in the season and in the greenhouse (or, in my case, the bathroom). Small seedlings and seeds will need to be watered with the rose fitted. Where a flat oval rose is fitted, this should be facing upwards. Larger transplants, seedlings and growing plants can be watered without the rose but take care not to wash the plant clean out of the ground. Water gently round the plant, not onto it.

Hosepipes mean fewer trips to the tap but are the first watering system to be disallowed in a drought. Hoses are used either hand-held or connected to an automatic watering system (see below). Connectors for hose ends are available, similar in design to the rose on a watering can. These break up the flow to give an effect similar to rain. Other devices allow you to turn on a jet or a spray by quick adjustment.

Automatic watering The problem with cans and hosepipes is that you have to be there all the time. Sprinklers do the job for you, needing only to be moved every two hours or so.

Such watering is very wasteful as much of the soil may not be occupied by plants and paths are better kept dry. Not all watering systems rely on the overhead rain principle. Water technology is improving rapidly and new systems operate underground, supplying water only as plants need it. A permeable hose is laid 5 cm (2 in) or more under the soil and connected to a small tank supplied by the mains water supply. As plant roots suck water out of the soil so the pipe releases more to replace it by a natural process called osmosis. In this way a row of plants can be supplied with exactly the right amount of water with no fuss and no waste. An older, well-tried and cheap system is the seep-hose. This is a flat hose laid on the surface along a row of plants. Water seeps out at low pressure through a stitched seam, thus supplying the plants but not unoccupied soil.

All these methods have their uses. A row of young seedlings can be watered by watering can but a young, emergent lawn is best served by a sprinkler or sprayed hose. The important thing is to save life-giving water.

WHEN TO WATER

A soil supplied with ample humus holds water very well. Once plants have reached into this soil with their roots they need much less watering. Seeds and seedlings, however, have to rely on the moisture in the top few centimetres (or even millimetres) of soil and they will need water every day, if the soil surface is dry, until they are strong enough to cope on less. This will be when they have two or three sets of "true" leaves showing (seed leaves are first to appear and are simpler and noticeably different).

As a general rule, the larger a plant is, the less watering it needs. For, although it has more leaves to feed, it has more roots to find water deeper in the soil. If plants begin to wilt you may suspect a shortage of water. The best check is to push a finger or trowel into the soil and see for yourself. If the soil at root level is damp then the wilting is caused by pest or disease and no amount of water will revive it.

Wind and sun quickly remove water from the soil's surface, especially if they occur together. In such conditions the best time to water is in the cool of the evening when the water will have a chance to percolate. In unheated greenhouses the ideal time for watering is determined by the outside temperature. On cold, dark days water is best applied, if at all, before midday. It has a cooling effect, and cold damp soil and wet leaves in the still environment of a greenhouse encourage disease. On hot sunny days you may need to water pots and trays more than once with a final check in the evening.

HOW MUCH WATER?

A regularly watered row of seedlings will need only topping up. A 10-litre (2-gallon) canful will be enough for 9 m (30 ft) of row, possibly more. Make sure that you have given enough by poking a finger into the watered soil to see how far it has penetrated.

Very dry soil will gain no benefit at all from this kind of light sprinkling. A soil that has become very dry will need at least 10 litres to each m^2 (2 gallons per yd^2) to wet it thoroughly. Plants growing in soil that is watered insufficiently tend to root closer to the surface to make use of the water available there. This makes them even more prone to drought when the supply dries up.

WATERING CHECKLIST

- Feed the soil with plenty of compost or manure (see p.31). Organic matter soaks up water and releases it slowly to thirsty plants.

- Use mulches round growing plants wherever possible (see p.35). Apply the mulch to damp, warm soil.

- Before watering, check with your finger or a trowel whether you really need to. The surface may be dry but there may be plenty of water below, especially if the soil is well manured.

- Seeds and tiny seedlings have short roots that have not yet penetrated far. These need watering daily in dry weather. Larger plants can manage with much less. Deep-rooting vegetables such as parsnips and carrots need very little once they are growing strongly.

- Newly planted shrubs and trees will need careful monitoring for water shortage during their first season. Older trees and shrubs can usually cope without water except in exceptionally prolonged dry spells of several months.

- If the soil is very dry to a depth of 30 cm (1 ft) or more, it will take at least 10 litres/m^2 (2 gallons/yd^2) to wet it through.

- Water late in the day unless frost is forecast. Sunshine evaporates surface water; starlight doesn't.

Chapter 8
BUILDING A NEW GARDEN

What Should I Grow?

N O TWO GARDENERS will have exactly the same plans for a plot. Many will be drawn to gardening simply by a desire to do something positive with the bit of ground outside the back door; others will have a compelling ambition to produce the biggest leeks in the county; others may long for the forgotten flavours of garden fresh fruit and vegetables. Unless you are aggressively ambitious, I suggest that you start with something relatively simple to enable you to get used to the way plants grow and to give yourself time to learn more. It is important for your morale to chalk up a few successes.

In general it is preferable to design a garden in detail before starting work. However, your first garden can be like a blackboard with exercises and experiments tried in different corners. Your first stone wall may collapse or your shrubs be too close together; your compost heap may be in quite the wrong place; the flower colours may clash horribly. Some of the most successful gardens have evolved slowly and no garden is ever completed.

Learning to look after the soil is the most important lesson. Growing vegetables and annual flowers and making compost will give you some good basic experience from which to expand. However, it is best to include flowering plants if you are concentrating on growing vegetables, because these help to attract beneficial creatures that feed on or parasitize pests (see p.118). You may abandon the vegetables later in favour of some other passion, but the value of these early lessons will not be lost.

Planning the Plot

The previous owner of your very first garden may have been an assiduous and competent gardener and left you a legacy of fine grass, exuberant borders and richly nurtured soil. On the other hand you are more likely to be faced with a knee-high jungle of coarse growth which defiantly disguises a rubbish tip of rubble, waste concrete, plastic bags and lemonade bottles. Hitch up your sinking morale and be comforted. It is surprising how much you can achieve in a short time.

Garden design is a subject too large to cover in any depth in this book. The list of further reading on p.153 refers you to a number of useful relevant books. My advice to any beginner is to start with a very simple plan. Achieving this will give you a chance to get to know some plants and acquire a few skills before you venture into more ambitious territory.

The sections that follow offer advice on how to construct a garden once you have established a plan.

Stages of Construction

Your first "blank page" of garden can be daunting. What do you tackle first? If you follow this simple sequence you should find that you are not undoing work that you have just completed.

1. Clear away all the old fridges, car tyres, rusting corrugated iron and other accumulated debris. Don't throw everything away on the tip. Some things can be useful for making compost bins and old bedsteads are marvellous for drying onions. Keep any bricks or concrete for hard core.
2. Take a soil sample and send it for analysis.
3. Measure the plot and draw up a plan.
4. Attend to drainage (see p.24).
5. Erect fences, lay paths and paved areas, build any retaining walls, plant perimeter hedges.
6. Clear the ground in preparation for planting. This could take some time (see p.125). Using a long-term light-excluding mulch will give you some time to recover from the work so far.

7. Prepare beds and lay lawns.
8. Carry out final planting.
9. Some plants may fail. Don't be too discouraged — try something else.

Erecting a Fence

(See notes on p.90 on choice of fence panel.)

EQUIPMENT REQUIRED:

- Two human beings and a still day
- String and pegs
- Spirit level
- Hammer and nails
- Length of wood of same length as one fence panel
- Spade for digging and mixing concrete (fork is useful if soil is hard)
- Concrete mixture, comprising 4 parts sand, 2 parts gravel, 1 part cement
- Rubble
- Three pieces of scrap timber about 2 m (6 ft) long
- Fence posts and panels (or rails and pales for a paling fence)
- Fence post caps

Note: For a 1.8-m (6-ft) high fence you will need fence posts 2.55 m (8½ ft) long. Fences of 1.5 m (5 ft) or less in height will need posts 67.5 cm (2ft 3in) longer than the fence height.

Boxed metal spikes (metposts) are available that can be driven into the ground as an alternative to digging and concreting. These do not hold well in all soils or on very exposed sites but can save a great deal of time and effort. For these you will need posts only a few centimetres taller than the fence panels.

Posts are normally 7.5 cm (3 in) square. If you are including a gate in your fence, it should hang on a 10-cm (4-in) square post.

METHOD:

1. Peg out one side of the fence with a very tight line. Remember that a fence post is 7.5 cm (3 in) wide. This line is going to be a guide to either the outer or inner edge of the fencing.

2. Dig out the first hole at a corner or one end to a depth of 60 cm (2ft) for a 1.8 m (6 ft) fence or 45 cm (18 in) for a lower fence, keeping topsoil and subsoil separate. The hole should be ideally not more than a spade and a half wide.

3. Place the first post in the hole. Using your spirit level, ensure that, when the post just touches the line, it is exactly upright.

4. Refill the hole with alternate layers of hard core and cement, finishing with a layer of cement 20–25 cm (8–10 in) below the surface soil level. Recheck that your post is upright. It is a good idea to brace this first post with lengths of scrap timber to ensure that it does not move. Ram the end of the braces a few centimetres into the soil and nail the other ends loosely to the post about two-thirds of the way up. They can be removed once the concrete has set.

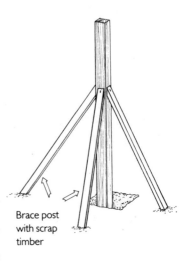

Brace post with scrap timber

5. Using your measuring stick, gauge the distance from this post to the next and dig out the second hole.

6. Fix your first panel to the first post by nailing it to the side facing down the line. Allow about 2 or 3 cm (1 inch) of ground clearance so the panel is not resting on the soil.

97

7. Drop the second post into the hole.

8. Measure the distance from the top of the panel to the top of the first post and make a mark the same distance from the top of the second post.

9. Holding the panel against the second post up to this mark, check with a spirit level along the top of the panel. You may have to refill the hole slightly with subsoil or take more out in order to set the post at the right depth.

10. Nail the panel to the post.

11. Check that the post is exactly upright when touching the line and re-fill the hole as in stage 4. On level ground you can continue like this round the plot. If your ground is sloping or undulating you will have to step the fence down or up.

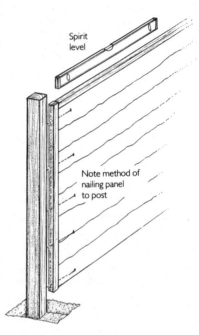

Spirit
level

Note method of
nailing panel
to post

Stepping Down:

12. Mark the next post with a line on one side as usual and fix the panel to it as in stages 9 to 11 above. Fix the next panel to the other side so that the bottom is just above the soil. Try to avoid too large a step each time. If the ground is gently sloping, it is better if panels are kept level until a step of 7.5−10 cm (3−4 in) is possible.

13. The next panels continue at the original distance from the top of the post until another step is necessary.

Stepping Up:

14. Each step up should be at least 7.5 cm (3 in) and, preferably, not more than 15 cm (6 in). Make a mark on

the next post at the new distance from the top (see illustration) and fix it to the panel at this new level. Set the post in the hole, ensuring that the panel is level along the top.

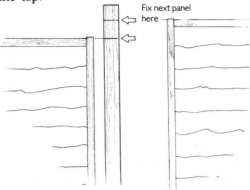

Fix next panel here

15. The next panel is then fixed at the original level from the top of the post.

Once the cement has set you can complete the process:

16. Fit a post cap on top of each post to protect the end grain from the weather.

17. Fill in the holes with topsoil and remove the subsoil. *The subsoil should not be spread around the garden on the surface.* It should be removed entirely or buried under topsoil.

Planting a Hedge

See p.152 for suitable hedging plants.

EQUIPMENT REQUIRED:

- Hedging plants: one for each 60 cm (2 ft) of row — but allow a few spares
- Canes
- String and pegs
- Spade, fork and trowel; wheelbarrow
- Roll of thin-gauge horticultural black polythene or newspaper with straw or hay mulch
- Manure and organic fertilizers if the soil is poor

METHOD:

1. Mark the line of your hedge with canes to give you an idea of how it is going to look. Canes are easier to move than growing shrubs.

2. Once you are satisfied, mark out a strip one metre (approx. 1 yard) wide with your pegs and string.

3. Rotovate or dig over this strip in early autumn, incorporating any turf or weeds growing on the surface. If the soil is poor or badly structured (see p.22), work in some compost or manure at this stage. Your soil analysis (p.156) will tell you what other organic fertilizers may be necessary. If you are using wild species of hedge plant native to your area you do not need a rich soil.

4. The greatest problem for your new hedge will be shortage of water and competition from weeds. This can be overcome by mulching with either black polythene or old newspaper. New polythenes are becoming available which are entirely biodegradable. These are obviously preferable.

5. If you are using polythene, lay it out over the cultivated strip and bury the edges. Newspaper mulch is laid *after* planting the hedge. Mulches should always be laid over moist soil.

6. The hedge can now be planted through slits in the mulch any time from November to late March. This is a knack that you will soon acquire. The soil has to be pushed aside under the polythene and then firmed back around the roots. It is a good idea to cover each slit with a handful of sand or to spread bark or woodchip mulch over the polythene to prevent the wind lifting and tearing the fabric.

7. If you are going to use newspaper as a mulch, the hedge is planted first. Spread newspaper at least six pages thick over the strip and cover the paper with wet straw or hay to prevent yesterday's news making today's local story as each page makes an independent passage through the neighbourhood. Remember to leave a space of a few centimetres round the stem of each plant stem to prevent mice or voles from chewing the bark in private.

LOOKING AFTER YOUR HEDGE

In the first year you will only need to water your hedge if it becomes dry under the mulch. At the end of the first year's growth clip back all side shoots by about one third but leave the central stem untouched.

As the hedge grows it will need trimming more often. Some hedge plants such as privet and *Lonicera nitida* (a shrubby honeysuckle) need clipping as often as once a month but others look tidy with a single annual trim. The central stem can be left uncut until it has reached the eventual height that you have chosen. Then it is cut back by 15-20 cm (6-8 in) to encourage it to make twiggy growth at the top.

The ideal hedge shape is wider at the base than the top. This allows sunlight to reach the maximum leaf area. Once the hedge is fully formed it can be clipped back quite tightly each year to maintain this shape without getting progressively taller and fatter.

You should not need to water your hedge after the first year unless there is a prolonged drought. Feeding, as always, should be a response to visible signs of poor growth or nutrient shortage but is rarely necessary for an established hedge.

Paths and Sitting-out Areas

Paths and patios are generally finished in gravel, concrete or paving. Laying paving and brick paviors is a skilled job and not recommended for first-time gardeners. Concrete is unattractive and fairly expensive. Gravel paths, however, are well within the capabilities of the keen beginner.

EQUIPMENT REQUIRED:

- Pegs and string
- Length of wood, measuring the width of the path
- Spirit level
- Spade and shovel
- Wheelbarrow
- Rubble or other suitable hard core base
- Edging material — preformed concrete edging, tannel-

ised wooden boards 15 cm (6 in) wide with 45 cm (18 in) pegs, "log-roll" edging or any other means of keeping soil and gravel apart

- Sand and gravel
- Pea gravel, Cotswold chippings or other fine-grade gravel finish
- Cement will be necessary if you are using concrete edging

METHOD:

1. Mark out the area with pegs and string.
2. Dig out the path or area to a depth of 20–22.5 cm (8–9 in).
3. Set the edging:
   a) Knock in a peg at either end of a run of edging and mark a point on each peg about 5 cm (2 in) above soil level (this represents the top of the edging).
   b) Tie a tight line to the pegs at these marks.
   c) If using wooden edging, attach it to its posts and knock in the posts so that the top of the edging aligns with the string.

   If concrete edging is being used, lay a layer of cement 15 cm (6 in) deep and wide and set the edger into the cement so that the top aligns with the string. Smooth over the cement so that it slopes away from the edging to allow water to run off.
   d) Use your measuring board to ensure that the other side of the path is always set at the same width and check with a spirit level to maintain an even height across the path.
4. Fill the path with rubble or other hard core to a point about 7.5 cm (3 in) from the top of the edging and ram it hard with a sledgehammer.
5. Lay a 5 cm (2 in) bed of coarse sand or sand and gravel over this, raking it well into any cracks to leave an even surface. Consolidate this with a roller or your heaviest pair of boots.
6. Lay the final gravel surface just 1.25 cm (½ in) deep and roll it again.

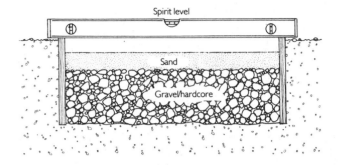

Note: A porous membrane can be laid to prevent any persistent weeds such as bindweed and dandelions from finding their way up through the hard core. This should be laid over the sand with a further 1.25 cm (½ in) of sand added before the final surface.

Stepping Stones

A simple and very pleasing effect can be created by placing pavers as stepping stones across a lawn. The irregular shape of York stone paving looks particularly attractive used in this way.

The distance between slabs is usually a source of heated disagreement, so I suggest that you proceed as follows:

1. Lay out the slabs across the lawn and ask all interested parties to test them out until a consensus is reached.

2. Cut the turf to fit the shape of each slab, remove it and dig out enough soil to accommodate the paver with 2 or 3 cm (1 in) to spare.

3. Place 2 or 3 cm (1 in) of sand in the hole, level it and drop in the slab.

4. Shuffle the slab until it has bedded in well and sits flush with the soil surface without rocking.

   Natural stone slabs often have an uneven base and you may need to adjust the sand underneath to settle the paver.

5. Brush some soil into any gaps around the pavers and the job is complete.

103

Laying a New Lawn

Lawns can be either sown or laid as turf. For the beginner, turfing is quicker and simpler although more expensive than growing from seed.

The first stages are identical with either method:

1. Attend to any drainage problems (see p.24) before starting.

2. Cultivate the whole area by rotovator or by forking it over. If you have any leafmould or spare compost, work it in at about one barrowful/5 m² (4½ yd²).

3. Using a hand cultivator (p.8) and rake, work the surface down to a fine tilth and as level as possible, working backwards across the plot.

4. Lightly tread the soil with a shuffling motion. This will gently compress the soil and prevent an uneven surface developing as it settles.

5. Rake the surface again, working in the opposite direction.

You are now ready for the final stages.

SEED

The best times of year to sow are April and September.

6. Using pegs and lines divide the plot into squares of 1 m (about 1 yd). This will enable you to sow the seed more accurately.

7. Working one square at a time, broadcast the seed evenly over the surface at the rate of 25 g/m² (¾ oz/yd²).
   Note: There are various mixtures of grass seed available. These will create lawns of different toughness and textures according to your plans. Choose the mixture carefully — a fine lawn cannot be used for playing regular games of football. The sowing rate quoted is for a general-purpose lawn mixture. Rates for other mixtures will vary.

8. Remove the lines and rake the seed in to leave as level a surface as possible.

9. Water this seedbed in dry weather with a sprinkler. The

seed should germinate in approximately two to three weeks. Keep everybody off, including the cat, until you start to mow it.

10. Do not be in a hurry to mow this new lawn. Allow it to grow at least 5 cm (2 in) tall before running a mower over it at the highest cut possible. Gradually reduce the cutting height over a period of weeks. It will be quite useful but not essential to use a light roller over the lawn a few days before the first cut. Weeds will germinate amongst the grass. Most will be annuals which will die out once mowing becomes regular.

TURFING

The best time of year is from October to March.

6. Mark the edges of the lawn area with a line — or canes if it is curving.

7. You should try not to walk on the raked surface while working. Have some boards ready to stand on as you work. Keep a bucket of good soil handy for tucking under thinner bits of turf or over small dips and depressions.

8. Butt the end of the first roll of turf against your line and roll out the turf. Feel the surface with your fingertips. Use some of the soil in the bucket to amend any irregularities or remove soil that creates a bump.

9. When you reach the other side cut off the turf with a lawn edger or spade along the edge marked by your line. If the turf does not quite reach the line, pull it up to the line and fit a slice from another roll into the gap created. Ensure an overlap at the edge where you are creating a curving edge for trimming later.

10. Using the back of a spade or, ideally, a fork, gently tamp the turf down. This is a gentle action — you are not breaking hard core.

11. Place the boards over the laid turf and start the next row.

12. Work across the plot in this way. Any joins that occur should be staggered so that no two in adjoining rows are aligned, in much the same way as bricks are laid.

13. Finally make a mixture of good soil and sharp sand in

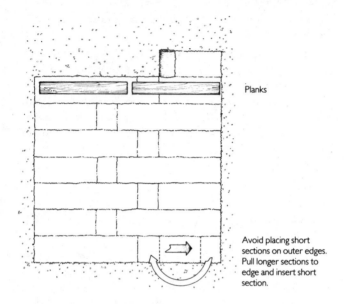

Planks

Avoid placing short sections on outer edges. Pull longer sections to edge and insert short section.

equal proportions and work this into all the cracks with the back of a rake.

14. Keep everybody off the lawn until it is growing well. It will need watering in dry weather until it has rooted well in to its new home.

15. A light roller at this stage will help to settle it and you can then start to mow it. The first cut should not be too short (see *Looking After Lawns*, p.72).

Flowerbeds and Borders

All the principles of soil preparation apply as much in the creation of flowerbeds as they do to the cultivation of food crops. In a new garden where heavy compaction has occurred after building work, you will need to double dig. You may even find that the subsoil excavated for the foundations has been plastered over the surface and thinly disguised with a smear of topsoil. In this instance you will need to buy in more topsoil. As always, it is worth having your soil analysed.

MARKING OUT

Straight lines and gentle curves both have merits suited to different styles. Whichever you choose, it is worth marking it with canes and leaving it for a few days to give you a chance to see if you like it.

Straight edges are easily marked with a pegged line but curves are more difficult. A hosepipe makes a good flexible edge and can be snaked round canes to fix it whilst you cut the edge.

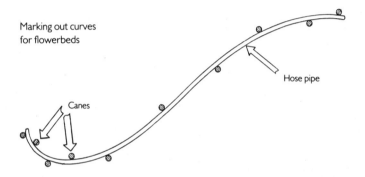

Marking out curves
for flowerbeds

Hose pipe

Canes

PREPARATION

If the plot is full of the more intractable weeds such as nettles, couch grass, docks and dandelions, it would be a good idea to give yourself a clean slate by killing all the growth. This can be done by double digging or using a light-excluding mulch (see p.126). If you are double digging, take the opportunity to incorporate some manure or compost and then sow an appropriate long-term or over-wintering green manure depending on the time of year (see p.38). All this requires patience but will repay your efforts in time.

Where the ground is under a fine lawn or not weedy, single digging alone may be satisfactory. Turf is best incorporated rather than stripped off, so that it adds to the organic matter content of the soil. Compost or manure at the rate of one barrowful to 4 m² (approx. 5 yd²) should also be dug in with the turf. This is best done in winter — you will then be able to plant it up during the spring.

PLANTING

Filling your beds with colour and shape is a matter of personal choice. They may be all annual flowering plants, all shrubs or mixtures of the two. Even some vegetables can look shapely and at ease amongst flowers, particularly the more ornamental lettuces, runner beans and artichokes. In practice, however, you will find that your choice is limited by certain physical factors:

- The pH of the soil and its nature (wet or dry)
- The amount of shading
- The shelter and aspect
- The size of the bed

When you are planting out, remember to allow each plant sufficient room to grow to its final size – a good gardening encyclopedia will give you this information. In the case of shrubs this will take several years to achieve and annual bedding plants can be used to fill the shrinking gaps in the intervening years.

The best time for planting shrubs is between November and March whilst annuals are usually planted out in May and June.

MAINTENANCE

Flowering plants do not generally need as much fertility as vegetables. On the other hand they cannot be expected to do well in a poor, starved soil. Mulches of organic matter are generally all that is necessary. Leafmould is excellent for this purpose as it does not supply large amounts of nutrients but does feed the soil. Where plants are clearly short of food, the appropriate organic fertilizer can be used (see p.40) but you should be aware that there may be other causes for poor growth (see p.43). Ornamental bark mulches will last for several years and have the added advantage of keeping moisture in and weeds out, whilst they slowly decompose to improve the soil.

Keep plants well watered until they are established and growing well.

Hoe off or dig out weeds periodically.

The Plants

DECIDING WHAT TO PLANT

Your garden will already have some limiting factors to be taken into account before you choose any plants. Chapter 7 explains some of the different conditions that need to be considered. Generally there is at least one plant for any place in a garden and the lists on pp.145–52 give some suggestions. You should also remember that some plants grow more upwards than outwards and others have the reverse habit. Tall plants, including some vegetables such as runner beans and Jerusalem artichokes, create shade which may affect parts of the garden that are at present regularly bathed in sunshine. Some surface-rooting plants, especially certain hedge plants such as privet and Lawson's and Leyland cypress, are particularly greedy for water and few plants will thrive near them. The following check list should help you avoid costly mistakes.

- Is the area prone to frost, especially late frosts?
- Is the plant exposed to the wind?
- How much sunshine will it get?
- Are there overhanging trees, which will drip on the plant in wet weather?
- Is the soil suitable? Is it acid or alkaline? Wet or dry?
- How tall and broad will the plant grow?
- Is it likely to spread vigorously?
- Does it have any resistance to pests or diseases (see p.120)?
- Does it need skilled pruning or special attention?
- When does it flower? You do not want all your colour to be over in a few weeks with nothing to follow.
- Does it have interesting foliage or bark?
- What colour are the flowers and foliage?

BUYING THE PLANTS

Where from? Garden centres generally stock a wide selection of trees, shrubs and herbaceous and annual bedding plants according to the season. Some nurseries specialize in certain plants and these will always offer you a better selection of varieties and, just as important, specific advice on the best conditions suited to different varieties. These specialists usually offer a mail order service and advertize through gardening publications and catalogues.

What to look for Not all garden centres and nurseries offer perfect specimens at honest prices. It is not so easy to shop around for plants as it is for clothing, but, if you have a chance, visit more than one garden centre or read several catalogues before making a final decision.

Look for:

- Healthy plants free from pests, disease and damage.
- A good root system. Plants bought in winter with bare roots should have a good fibrous root system. Plants in pots should not be pot-bound with a mat of roots protruding from underneath.
- A reasonable price. Prices vary enormously between one catalogue or garden centre and another.

Chapter 9
DEALING WITH DISASTERS: PESTS AND DISEASES

THE ARRIVAL OF the first hordes of spring-fevered insects can seriously deplete the beginner's reserves of enthusiasm. Steel your nerve and stand firm. Problems invariably occur. Most can be anticipated or avoided without resorting to a rain of death from a sprayer. There are many tricks, traps and wrinkles that can be employed to reduce pest and disease damage. Prevention is always better than cure and so foresight, combined eventually with experience, will be your principal weapon.

Unfortunately this book cannot cover all the specific pests and diseases of plants and their treatment. Other books do this in detail (see *Book List*, p.153) and should be used in conjunction with this one. My intention is to give you a general understanding of organic methods. Many of these, as you will see, have a much broader and more beneficial effect than a "which pest — which spray?" attitude.

What are Pests?

After millennia of evolution, the gardener is still no nearer to convincing his fellow creatures that garden plants are there purely for the enjoyment of humans and are not an open invitation to lunch. All those — with or without legs, large and small — that try to claim a share of your plants may be regarded as pests. Strict categorization is not possible and not every creature that crawls or looks menacing is a pest. Blackbirds, for example, will steal your fruit but they also feed on soil pests; earwigs can ruin some flowers but they are eager hunters of insects and their eggs; wasps can be a dreadful nuisance but they are hearty feeders on aphids and small caterpillars. There are, in addition, some creatures whose presence is almost entirely beneficial. It is worth getting to know these as many look decidedly unfriendly.

What is Disease?

Just as not everything that crawls or flies is a pest, so not all withering, wilting or wrinkles are caused by disease. Frost, wind and weather (see chapter 7) can all damage plants — as can gardeners.

Diseases are caused by fungi, bacteria or viruses. Fungi and bacteria need, in general, fairly specific conditions in order to establish themselves. The result appears in the form of rusts, mildews, rotting or moulds. A virus is something altogether more sinister. Although a plant is not usually killed by a virus, it is so weakened and enfeebled by the attack that it is rarely worth keeping. The symptoms of virus disease vary greatly but usually involve distorted and stunted growth, strange leaf colourings such as marbling, mottling or spots and, in the case of flowering and fruiting plants, poor cropping or few flowers. Viruses are spread most commonly by sap-sucking insects such as greenfly or on contaminated soil. Soil is regularly moved round the garden on tools and boots, so that an isolated attack can be spread unwittingly to other plants. Soil-borne viruses are, fortunately, less common than insect-borne ones.

Protecting Your Plants

HEALTHY LIVING
Healthy plants living in the right conditions in well-managed soil are much less likely to contract a disease and can cope with some pest damage. These conditions are covered in more detail in chapters 3, 4, 7 and 8.

THE MIXED GARDEN
The plot that contains only food plants is prone to all the problems experienced in the prairie monocultures that have spread across the farmed land of the developed world. Such

plots attract only pests. A more mixed garden, on the other hand, is home to a more varied wildlife. Here pests and their enemies live side by side, eventually reaching a balance where there are always some pests but rarely plagues and the predators are kept fat and happy. Most of the creatures that are helpful to the gardener need more than just a food source of insects to survive. See the chart on p.118. The following features all attract garden friends.

Anthocorid bug

Pond This need not be large. Preformed fibreglass ponds are readily available and not difficult to install. You will be surprised how quickly a pond becomes colonised. Ponds should not just be bowls of water but a genuine habitat with pond weed, water plants, a shallow ledge to allow easy access for frogs, and plants round the edge to give cover for the timid.

Lacewing larva

Attracts: Birds, frogs, toads, newts, dragonflies, damselflies and a host of other creatures including bees, which will come to drink.

Note: Goldfish eat spawn and tadpoles. Keep them separate.

Ladybird larva and pupa

113

Dry stone walls take skill to build well but making a small wall 75–90 cm (18 in–2 ft) high is much like doing a jigsaw. Perfect joins are not important as the idea is to create living space for other creatures.

Attract: Toads, frogs, slowworms, centipedes, spiders and occasionally nesting birds such as pied wagtails.

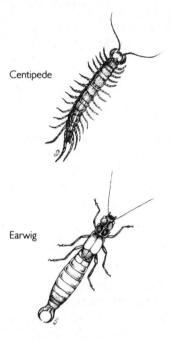

Centipede

Hedges (see p.99) make ideal nesting sites for many birds. Hedges of native and berrying plants also provide food. The dense litter that accumulates under a hedge is often sought out by hibernating hedgehogs.

Attract: Birds, hedgehogs, toads, beetles, predatory and parasitic insects.

Earwig

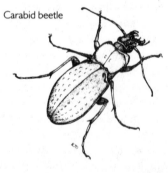

Birdtable, bird and bat boxes Many birds would not survive a hard winter without the help of humans. Not all birds eat insects, but many do, and without their appetites we would be virtually unable to garden.

Carabid beetle

Bats are in decline and need help. They feed on

Hoverfly larva eating aphid

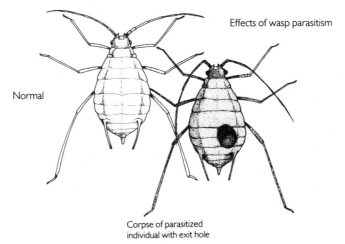

Effects of wasp parasitism

Normal

Corpse of parasitized
individual with exit hole

night-flying moths and insects, many of which are serious pests. A bat box fitted to the eaves of a house or on a tree can provide temporary roosting or nesting facilities for them.

Plants to attract Ladybirds are amongst just a few aphid-eating creatures that can manage on aphids alone. Most others need a source of nectar or pollen as well. In many cases, whilst the larvae feed on aphids, mites and other insects, the adults are nectar feeders and so are most likely to lay their eggs in pest colonies near suitable flowering plants. Not all the flowers attractive to gardeners attract beneficial insects. In general they need single, open flowers with short throats to suit their short tongues. Many modern varieties are known as "doubles" and have complex, frilly petal formations which do not suit these insects.

Slow worm

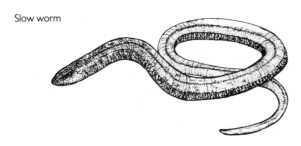

115

Some attractant flowering plants

★ See p.63 for explanation of terms

Latin Name	Common Name	Description	Height/spread (cm)
ANNUALS★			
Calendula officinalis	Pot marigold	Bright orange flowers	60 × 45
Convolvulus minor	Annual convolvulus	Open flowers in blue or pink with yellow throat	25 × 40
Echium vulgare	Viper's bugloss	Blue bell-shaped flowers	30 × 20
Esch-scholtzia californica	Californian poppy	Long-flowering yellow-orange poppies; self-seeds	45 × 30
Helianthus spp.	Sunflower	Giant yellow daisy	300 × 90 Dwarf form 120 × 90
Limnanthes douglasii	Poached egg flower	Early-flowering yellow and white; self-seeds	15 × 30
Nemophila insignis	Baby Blue-Eyes	Bright blue with white eye	25 × 25
Phacelia tanacetifolia	Phacelia	Spikes of violet flowers above feathery foliage; loved by bees	60 × 30
BIENNIALS★			
Angelica archangelica	Angelica	Round heads of small white flowers in spring; self-seeds	150 × 90
Verbascum bombiciferum	Mullein	Silvery woolly leaves; tall spikes studded with yellow flowers	150 × 60
Cichorium intybus	Chicory	Grown as vegetables; blue flowers in second year	90 × 95

Latin Name	Common Name	Description	Height/spread (cm)
PERENNIALS★			
Anaphalis spp.	Pearl everlasting	Tiny white flowers with yellow centre	45 spreading (dwarf form 20 cm)
Achillea spp.	Yarrow	Feathery foliage; flat heads of densely crowded flowers in white, pink or yellow	60 to 120 × 45 (depending on variety)
Aster novi-belgii	Aster	Daisy flowers in white, pink, red, blue; mildew-resistant	120 × 75
Chrysanthemum maximum	Shasta daisy	Large white daisies	90 × 60
Eryngium maritimum	Sea holly	Spiny blue flowers	60 × 60
Foeniculum vulgare	Fennel	A herb; feathery foliage, handsome dark form available	120 × 60
Myrrhis odorata	Sweet Cicely	White flowers in flat heads in spring; sweetly scented	60 × 60

There are a great many types of beetle that feed on soil-living grubs and eggs including slugs. Centipedes have similar taste. These need ground-cover plants to give them protection from the sun and predatory enemies.

Ladybirds emerge from hibernation early in the year with an urgent need for food. Their main food source is aphids and amongst the earliest to emerge are nettle aphids. A rough patch of garden with some carefully managed nettles will give your ladybirds a fast food snack to tide them over until the aphids turn up on the roses and broad beans.

Attract: Hoverflies, parasitic wasps, lacewings, predatory mites, beetles, ladybirds.

117

Beneficial creatures and their benefits

Animal/Insect	Feeds on
Bats	Moths and other night-flying insects
Birds	Flying and soil-living insects
Hedgehogs	Slugs and other soil-living creatures
Frogs	Insects and some slugs
Toads	Insects
Spiders	Flying insects, including many aphids★
Slow worms	Slugs and other soil-living creatures
Beetles (rove, carabid etc.)	Eggs, larvae, pupae in soil, slugs
Ladybirds	Aphids
Hoverflies	Larvae eat aphids
Parasitic flies and wasps	Lay eggs inside aphids or caterpillars
Lacewings	Larvae eat aphids
Dragonflies/damselflies	Flying insects
Anthocorids	Aphids, mites, midges, weevils
Earwigs	Eggs and small larvae
Wasps	Aphids, small caterpillars
Predatory mites	Red spider mites
Centipedes (distinguished from millipedes by having one pair of legs not two per segment)	Slugs and other soil-living pests

★ Aphid is a general term for a family of small, sap-sucking pests. You will also hear them referred to as "greenfly" or "blackfly". Whitefly are not aphids.

SEED SOWINGS

Starting the season There is no official ribbon-cutting, fan-fared start to the gardening year. Even climatic maps can be misleading with our unpredictable weather patterns. Even if a few warm days and twittering birds suggest the onset of spring, do not be tempted to sow too early in the year. Experience will show you that later sowings easily catch up and generally germinate better, with fewer losses to fungal diseases, slugs and other pests. Apart from the hardier vegetables such as broad beans and leeks, outdoor sowings are best left until the soil warms in April unless you live in the warmer parts of the country. Wherever possible, start plants indoors and transplant them after hardening off (see p.69).

Sowing to miss the pests Much is known about the lifecycle of pests. Some have only one generation each year. As eggs or pupae, pests are inactive. By coinciding sowings to take advantage of this, you can sometimes grow a crop to harvest before serious damage is done. Carrots sown in June, for example, do most of their growing between peak periods of carrotfly activity. A good book on pest control will tell you when to expect trouble.

BRINGING IN TROUBLE

There are some very persistent pests and diseases that can survive in soil without a host for a very long time. Be wary of accepting free plants over the fence unless you are certain that your neighbour's garden is free of onion white rot, clubroot (which affects members of the cabbage family), potato eelworm, strawberry red core and other problems. The list is long enough to make the asking an embarrassment, whilst the damage to your plants will be more embarrassing. Any plant with soil attached to its roots could be a potential hazard unless you are confident of the source. Bare-rooted transplants from garden centres and nurseries are not likely to be contaminated.

ROTATING CROPS

(For more information on crop rotation see p.45).

It is sound practice to ensure that plants from the same family do not follow each other year after year in the vegetable plot. The same applies to beds cleared of old strawberries, raspberries, roses or any other uniform planting. These latter plots need at least one year under a green manure (see p.37) in order to recover fertility before they can be reused for the same crop.

RESISTANT PLANTS

It pays to read catalogues carefully. There are an increasing number of plant varieties which have been specially bred to be less susceptible to damage from specific pests or diseases. By choosing to grow these you will be reducing the likelihood of problems. There are snapdragons that resist rust, a gooseberry that is virtually immune to mildew, lettuces untroubled by root aphid and roses less damaged by blackspot.

TRAPS AND PROTECTIVE BARRIERS

Some pests do not get eaten and will not be deterred. The answer to these is either to catch them out (the poor things do not have large brains) or keep them out.

Traps can be primitive or sophisticated. One of the simplest is a small pile of old lettuce leaves placed on the soil and covered with a slate, stone or roof tile. Slugs and snails soon home in on these as a daytime refuge. They can then easily be collected and despatched.

The winter moth female has to climb an apple or pear tree to reach its egg-laying site. A 10-cm (4-in) band of special grease or greased paper will catch her *en route*. Prepared greasebands can easily be bought and cost little − do not be tempted to use car grease, which may kill or damage the tree.

The more sophisticated traps make use of natural stimulant odours given off by moths either to attract a mate or raise the alarm. A number are available to commercial growers but the only one so far produced for garden use is the codling moth trap. Female codling moths lay eggs in apple and pear trees that hatch and grow into the familiar maggot, or more familiar half-maggot, in the apple. The trap contains a capsule that attracts male moths to their death on a sticky board. Fewer males mean fewer fertilized eggs.

Barriers quite simply prevent pests reaching a crop. The most obvious example is the netting used on a fruit cage to keep birds from getting to the harvest first. This idea can be adapted to protect cabbages from the caterpillars of the cabbage white butterfly. A mesh size of 1 cm (½ in) is needed to achieve this.

Even smaller mesh is required to keep out the tiny fly responsible for the maggots that tunnel their way through carrots. *Carrotfly barriers* are now quite a common sight. A very fine mesh net is either fixed to posts 1 m (3 ft) apart round the carrots or stretched onto frames that are then attached to posts. The barrier should be at least 75 cm (2½ ft) high and not more than 1.2 m (4 ft) wide (see illustration).

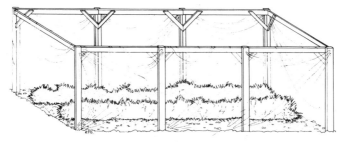

Carrotfly barrier

The cabbage rootfly lays its eggs on the soil near the stem of a cabbage or related plant. The hatched grubs burrow into the soil and then invade the roots. *Cabbage mats* can be made from carpet underlay cut into 12.5 cm (5 in) squares with a slit to the centre. When these are in place, the rootfly cannot find soil close enough to the stem. In addition predatory beetles hide under the mats to pick up any eggs that are laid.

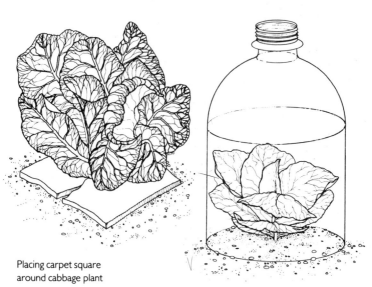

Placing carpet square
around cabbage plant

Plastic bottle with base removed,
placed around plant to
prevent slugs attacking it

121

Plastic drink bottles can also be used as barriers. Cut off the bottoms, remove the screw caps and push them into the ground round young plants, which would otherwise fall prey to slugs or cutworms. Susceptible seedlings include French beans, lettuces, sunflowers, Chinese cabbage, parsley. Larger 5-litre (1-gallon) bottles can be brought into service for courgettes and pumpkins. When the plants are growing well and becoming cramped, remove the bottle. Check periodically that you have not trapped a slug *inside* the bottle.

COMPANION PLANTING

Companion planting has more status than statistics. The idea of plants having a beneficial or protective influence on each other is attractive and seductive. There is, however, no sound supporting evidence for the majority of claims. Beginners should not rely on this as a method of plant protection — but it can be fun to experiment.

A BEADY EYE

Many problems race out of control simply because they are not spotted in time. Beginners cannot expect to recognize symptoms accurately but will soon learn what looks "right" and what does not. Recourse to a good book should tell you what you have seen. Regular inspection of your garden will help you learn quite quickly (in gardening terms) how plants grow, how they should look, when certain pests arrive, what damage they inflict and what diseases to anticipate. Nipping out a slightly mildewed shoot could prevent a whole tree succumbing. Blackfly tend to infest the growing tips of broad beans first. Pinching out these tips will delay or even prevent rapid colonization. Vigilance may pick up early signs of virus — your foresight could save you the loss of a whole crop.

Sprays for Organic Gardens

Not even sprays acceptable in organic gardens are harmless. Proper care should always be taken and the correct product used for the problem. Spraying should always be used as a last resort and you should always opt for the least potent option first.

SOME CAUTIONS:

- Read the label and follow the instructions carefully.
- Use a product suitable for the pest or disease.
- Keep all sprays away from children.
- Do not spray on windy days.
- Clean your sprayer after use.
- Do not store left-over spray mixes.
- Store preparations in their original containers or in well-labelled bottles.
- Organic pesticides kill by contact. Unaffected parts of the plant will not benefit from a spraying.
- Be aware that some organic pesticides can kill bees or beneficial insects. If bees are working a crop, spray only if absolutely necessary and then in the evenings after the bees are safely in the hive.
- Bordeaux mixture and sulphur can harm some varieties of apple and gooseberry or other plants at certain stages of their growth.

SPRAYS FOR PESTS

Soft soap An old-fashioned vegetable soap. Mix with rain water or soft water for best effect to kill aphids. Kills by contact. Also used to help other sprays to stick to leaves effectively as a "wetting agent". Very safe.

Insecticidal soap A more efficient vegetable-derived soap spray. Kills by contact.

Used for: aphids, whitefly, red spider mite, leaf-hoppers, blackcurrant leaf midge and some slug-worms.

Safe for humans, animals, bees and most beneficial insects. Can harm ladybird larvae. Can damage young, tender growth.

Derris (Rotenone) Extracted from plant roots. Powder or liquid concentrate. Kills by contact or if eaten.

Used for: aphids, caterpillars, sawfly larvae, cane midge, red spider mite, raspberry beetle, flea beetle and thrips.

Poisonous to fish, bees, ladybirds, anthocorid bugs and some parasitic wasps. Also harmful to humans and animals in concentration. Breaks down rapidly.

Pyrethrum A flower extract, nowadays usually available mixed with derris, which is acceptable, or with the chemical piperonyl butoxide, which is not. It is not possible to buy pure pyrethrum at the time of writing. Kills by contact.

Used for: aphids, flea beetles, small caterpillars (large caterpillars can survive it).

Poisonous to fish and some types of ladybird.

Safe for humans and animals.

Bacillus thuringiensis Bacteria in powder form which is made into a spray to cause disease in many, but not all, caterpillars. Harmless to all other creatures. Kills when eaten. Mixed with soft soap or some other "wetting agent" (see above).

Used for: caterpillars of butterflies and moths that feed on cabbage family. Other caterpillars vary in ability to resist it.

SPRAYS FOR DISEASES

It is mainly the fungal diseases that can be treated with organically acceptable sprays. In general the organic sprays are more useful as a preventative measure rather than a cure. It is not a sound principle to spray "just in case". Where a problem cannot be controlled or avoided by better gardening methods, one of the sprays may be worth considering.

Bordeaux mixture A mixture of copper and hydrated lime.

Caution: Copper is a trace element (see p.31) and excessive amounts in the soil can poison plants. Harms some plants.

Poisonous to fish and animals but not bees.

Used to prevent: potato blight, fruit tree cankers, leaf spot of gooseberries and currants, downy mildew on grapes.

Sulphur Use in powder form or in solution with water.

Caution: Several varieties of apple and gooseberry are harmed by it. Plants are particularly susceptible in frosty weather and when young.

Used to prevent: all types of powdery mildew and some rusts, apple and pear scab, gall mite in blackcurrants.

Chapter 10
WEEDS

What are Weeds?

PLANTS ARE PROGRAMMED genetically to reproduce. Many cast seed generously in order to achieve this and much of it falls in places where it is unwelcome. This is true not only of wild plants but also of cosseted cultivated ones. In fact we are happy for our colourful annuals to self-seed in the garden, saving us several packets of seed, not to mention potting compost and anxious moments awaiting successful germination. Other seedlings are less acceptable members of the garden community, some producing long, tough taproots or extensive ramifications of roots plunging farther down into the soil than any fork can reach. These latter include bindweed which can produce a shoot from any piece of root left in the ground.

Any plant growing where you do not want it becomes a weed. Some are more easily dealt with than others. There is even a case for leaving a part of your garden less scrupulously tidied for some wild weeds to live and seed. These should help in the organic gardener's aim for an environment that attracts beneficial insects and other creatures. Weeds in the beds and borders should not be tolerated, however, as they will be using up water and nutrients needed by your flowers and food crops.

Getting rid of weeds

CLEARING GROUND
Land that is going to become a flowerbed, vegetable plot or fine lawn needs first to be cleared of waist-high weeds. It is

extremely difficult to remove tough perennial weeds from amongst growing plants, so a clean soil makes a good start. The first task is to cut down and rake off any tall, dense growth and stack it somewhere to rot down. The ground can then be cleared either by cultivation or by covering. There is no need to slice off any turf from grassy areas. This can be killed out or cultivated under, saving the valuable active top few centimetres of soil and the potential soil-improving organic matter as the grass and weeds rot.

BY CULTIVATION

Double digging (see p.58) is an old and tried way of clearing ground. Weeds are buried so far down that they cannot regrow. Many persistent weeds are killed in this way but it is best to discard dock, dandelions, thistle and other tough roots as you come across them. If left to dry out they can be safely mixed into the compost heap.

Ground treated in this way in autumn or winter can be planted up in spring. However, it may pay to give the plot a summer under a green manure crop (see p.37) to give you another chance at any determined survivors.

Rotovating If soil is regularly churned with a rotovator in dry weather during the growing season, weeds are regularly up-rooted and dry out. By the third or fourth time most of the weeds will have died and any seedlings will be ploughed under. Any that are left can easily be dug out by hand.

The disadvantage of this system is that the ground is left bare for a long period and plant food could be washed out by heavy rain. The plot should be planted up in autumn or overwintered under a green manure (see p.37) and planted up in spring.

BY COVERING

If plants are starved of light they cannot survive. By covering land with a light-excluding material it is possible to clear it very efficiently. There are some mulching materials made especially for this purpose but others cost nothing and are easily obtained. Any of the following are suitable:

- Black polythene. Thin-gauge is sufficient. Bury the edges and weight down overlaps with sand or bricks.

- Woven or spun-bonded soil cover. See also *Growing through mulches* on p.128.
- Old carpets held down by bricks or wire pegs.
- Cardboard held down by planks or wedges of old hay.

Carpet sections stapled to ground

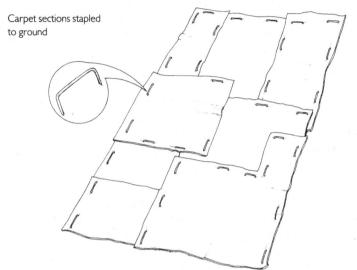

WEEDS IN BEDS AND BORDERS

Wherever there is bare soil, weed seeds will take advantage. In cultivated soil there are also many thousands of ungerminated seeds waiting to be thrown to the surface by digging. No matter how assiduous you are, there will always be weeds in your garden. The sudden green speckling of spring-time soil with seedling opportunists need not alarm you. There are simple efficient ways of dealing with these.

Hoeing The hoe (see p.9) is ideal for slicing off weeds between rows of crops or in flowerbeds. Use it when the soil surface is dry. Regular hoeing in dry weather in spring and early summer should keep beds and borders tidy for the season.

Some vegetable seeds, such as parsnip, are very slow to germinate. A few radishes sown along the row will germinate quickly to show you where the row is. You may then hoe between rows with confidence if weeds come up before the crop does.

127

Hand weeding with a hand fork or border fork will get to those weeds growing between tightly spaced plants where a hoe might do some damage. The close spacing on vegetable beds eventually creates a complete canopy of leaves that discourages weed growth. Some deep-rooting or persistent weeds such as docks or couch grass will regrow if their top growth is hoed off. These are, therefore, best removed by hand.

Growing through mulches Mulches (see p.35), either of organic matter or man-made materials, can be used very effectively to suppress weeds and conserve water round growing plants. Organic mulches have the additional benefit of feeding the soil. Listed below are some of the common materials used for weed control with some suggested uses.

Materials laid first; plants set out afterwards through holes

- Black polythene − hedges, trees.
- Woven or spun-bonded soil cover − strawberries, shrubs. (This kind of material may need covering with ornamental bark or woodchip mulch to slow deterioration caused by sunlight.)
- Biodegradable recycled paper mulch − annual vegetable crops such as cabbages, leeks, French beans, or between runner bean poles where hoeing is awkward.

Materials laid round growing plants

These materials should be applied to damp soil from the end of April onwards to ensure that the soil has already warmed. Mulches should not be laid round tiny seedlings. Slugs may accumulate under the mulch for night sorties on the seedlings.

- Shredded prunings − flower beds, shrub borders, trees and hedges.
- Ornamental bark or woodchip mulches − flowerbeds, shrub borders, trees and hedges.
- Lawn mowings − between rows of vegetables.
- Hay, straw − fruit bushes, strawberries, potatoes (on the no-dig system (p.84), courgettes, marrows and pumpkins.
- Newspaper (covered with straw or hay) − should be at least 8 pages thick and overlapping; avoid coloured

Newspaper (at least
8 layers thick)
covered with straw

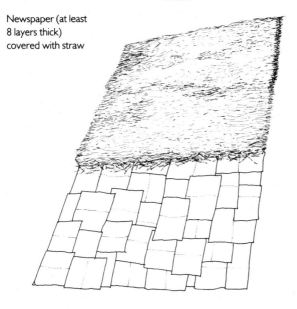

print. Newly planted fruit trees and bushes, raspberries, widely spaced vegetables in very weedy ground.

Neglected beds are often a tangle of beauty and beasts. Where couch grass, bindweed or ground elder have invaded, there is little option but to start again as follows.

In autumn lift out all the cherished plants, carefully disentangling all weed roots. Plant these out temporarily in an unused patch of clean soil. They can be quite close together. Very large shrubs do not transplant easily and will have to be sacrificed.

Fork over the entire area, removing all weed roots. Work in manure or compost at the rate of one barrowful to every 4–5m² (approx 4–5 yd²). If you are satisfied that you have been efficient, return the plants at the correct spacing. If you are in doubt use a green manure during the following summer and replant in autumn after digging in the green manure.

If the bed is seriously infested and especially if bindweed is present, cover the area with a weed-suppressing mulch (see *Clearing Ground*, p.125) for the following year and then proceed as above.

129

WEEDS IN PATHS AND PAVING

Although gravel does not support luxuriant plant life, seeds will germinate in it and occasionally more persistent weeds will encroach from nearby soil and try to colonize. Cracks in paving are rarely weed-free for ever. Plants are opportunists and any space or crevice makes a home, so that old neglected paths and paved areas can become heavily choked with tough weeds. In this instance the best policy is to swallow hard and remake the path. Such drastic measures are not usually necessary and simple tools and techniques can keep paths clean.

Specialist tools for weeding between paving stones can be bought but an old stainless steel cutlery knife makes a cheaper alternative. The hilt makes a useful fulcrum for gouging out more reluctant seedlings.

The ever-useful hoe will keep gravel relatively free of weeds. Dandelions occasionally pose a deeper-rooting problem and these will need to be prised out with a knife or garden fork.

Flame weeders kill weeds with a searing flame that bursts plant cells. Grasses and deep-rooting perennial weeds are only temporarily set back but can be progressively weakened by regular flaming. Annual weeds are killed instantly. Flame weeders need safe handling not only to protect humans but also to avoid burning cherished plants close to paths or igniting dry mulches. Ideal conditions are damp, windless days after rain.

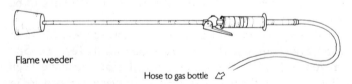

Flame weeder

Hose to gas bottle

WEEDS IN LAWNS

It is quite usual for weed seeds to germinate amongst grass seedlings in newly sown lawns. The majority of these are annuals which will die out after the first year as regular mowing cuts off flowerheads and prevents seeding. Further information on weeds in lawns is on p.78.

Some Common Weeds

The following list of weeds and their treatment is not
all-inclusive but covers most of the common ones. You will
soon learn to recognize the appearance of many of them.

Control	Weed
By hoe or hand:	all small seedlings
	bittercress
	chickweed
	fathen
	groundsel
	herb Robert
	shepherd's purse
	thistles, annual
	speedwell
By digging out	all established weeds
	grasses
	buttercups
	clovers
	dandelion — whole root
	dock — at least top 10 cm (4 in) of root
	ground elder
	lesser celandine★
	oxalis★
	★ (make sure you remove all the tiny bulbils, each of which will make a new plant)
By light-excluding mulch:	any large weedy area of previous group
	creeping thistle
	bindweed
	marestail

Chapter 11
GARDEN WORK THROUGH THE SEASONS

G ARDEN WORK HAS NO precise calendar. Spring starts sooner in the south and frost-free days for northerners can end abruptly in early September. Remember that later sowings will often catch up with untimely sowings made in a fever of enthusiasm into cold, unwelcoming soil. The following notes are intended as a reminder and approximate guide, not as a complete work schedule. It is laid out by seasons rather than months to allow for climatic variations across the country.

Winter

This is the quiet season when there is little growth taking place. It is a time for preparation and planning.

GENERAL
- Keep off the soil especially in wet conditions.
- Check through catalogues and order seeds and plants.
- Clean up pots and seedtrays ready for spring.

VEGETABLES AND FRUIT
In early winter:
- Dig compost trenches and fill them gradually through the season with kitchen waste.
- Hardy vegetables such as cabbages, Brussels sprouts, leeks, parsnips, salsify, scorzonera can be left outside and harvested as needed. Swedes and celeriac should be brought in to store as should carrots in colder areas.
- Check through fruit and vegetables already in store and discard rotten ones.

- Prune gooseberries, redcurrants, apples and pears.
- Protect buds on gooseberries from sparrows and bull-finches with netting.
- Plant out rhubarb and fruit trees and bushes.

In late winter:

- Set out seed potatoes in trays indoors to sprout before planting out in spring.
- Plant out shallots, and also garlic if not done in late autumn.
- Make earliest sowings indoors in trays: onions, broad beans, Brussels sprouts, early lettuce.
- Cut out autumn-fruiting raspberry canes and cut back tips of summer-fruiting ones to the top wire — about 1.2–1.5 m (4–5 ft).

TREES, SHRUBS, FLOWERS AND LAWNS

- Carry out any construction work: paths, walls, etc.
- Plant trees, shrubs when soil is not too wet or frozen.
- Leave dead flowerheads of herbaceous perennials for birds to eat seed. Cut down and compost remains.
- Rake up fallen leaves and stack for leafmould.
- Lay turf and repair lawns when soil is not frozen or very wet.
- Carry out winter pruning of shrubs such as buddleia, dwarf spiraea and summer-flowering clematis. Clip winter-flowering heathers once flowering is over.
- Sow sweet peas indoors in individual pots.

THE NEW GARDEN

- Buy basic tool set.
- Send off soil sample for analysis.
- Clear away all rubbish, cut down dense weed growth and stack to rot down.
- Build compost bins and prepare worm bins.
- Prepare garden plan and order plants/seeds.
- Carry out garden construction: fences, walls, pond, paths, terraces.

- Mark out beds and vegetable plots with string and canes.
- Plant out any bare-rooted trees and shrubs.
- Prepare lawn area if laying turf. Lay turf when soil is not frozen or too wet.

In late winter (or early spring):

- Prepare all ground on which you plan to grow plants or crops during the year. (This does not apply to plots which will need clearing with a light-excluding mulch.) Dig in green manures where hardy annuals, perennials or early vegetables are to be planted.

Spring

Spring is a busy season of high expectations, hopeful sowings and anxious waiting. A few warm days in March do not necessarily indicate the start of spring. Wait until the soil is warmer before committing seed to the ground.

GENERAL

In early spring:

- Dress soil with lime, compost, manure, leafmould according to its needs.
- Dig in overwintered green manures.

Throughout the season:

- Weeds will start to pop up everywhere. Keep working round with a hoe.
- Watch out for pests and diseases.
- Keep young seedlings and seeds watered until growing well.
- Mulch warm damp soil round growing crops where appropriate.
- Worm bin can now be stationed outside.

VEGETABLES AND FRUIT

In early spring:

- Sow quick-maturing green manures such as mustard and phacelia on vacant land where plantings will be late — i.e. before late cabbages, kale or tender crops such as courgettes, climbing beans and sweetcorn.

- Prepare seedbeds (see p.107) and cover with polythene to protect from heavy rain or drying winds and sun.

- Plant out all seed potatoes during late March and April.

- Protect emerging shoots from frost by earthing up or covering with horticultural "fleece", net curtains, old sheets, hessian sacks or similar material.

- Check fruit trees and bushes for pests and diseases.

- Hoe off unwanted shoots of raspberries that emerge away from the row.

- Dig in green manures prior to early plantings (early cabbage, lettuce, onion sets). Plant out onion sets.

- Start sowings indoors and outside. Check seed packets or gardening books for correct timing.

In mid-spring:

- At least two weeks prior to planting, dig in, hoe off or mulch out all remaining green manures where late plantings or sowing will be made.

- Ensure all overwintered crops are cleared away and composted once harvesting is completed.

- Continue sowing seeds. Prick out and pot on as necessary.

- Harden off all indoor-raised plants before setting them out.

- Pinch out blossoms on newly planted fruit trees and bushes.

- Tuck straw round strawberry plants and under fruit tresses when fruitlets start to form.

- Start thinning raspberry canes.

- Continue checking for pests and diseases.

In late spring:

- Continue sowing seeds, pricking out and potting on.

135

- Continue planting out in favourable conditions. Wait until frosts are over before setting out tender plants. Water in transplants and keep watered until established.
- Mulch fruit and vegetables as appropriate when soil is moist.
- Thin out seedlings in outdoor sowings.
- Keep plots weeded and watered when needed.
- Continue regular inspections for pests and diseases.
- Thin out fruitlets on apples, pears and plums.
- Start tying in canes of blackberries and hybrid berries.
- Net strawberries and other vulnerable fruits.
- Remove runners from strawberries.
- Prune plums and cherries.

TREES, SHRUBS, FLOWERS AND LAWNS
In early spring:

- Sow all annuals from early spring onwards. Check seed packets or gardening books for timing.
- Start weeding through beds.
- Divide clump-forming perennials if too large.
- Lift, divide and replant dense clumps of snowdrops whilst leaves are still green. Do not remove leaves.
- Plant out sweet peas with supporting canes.
- Prune roses.
- Feed lawns if necessary and start mowing on a high cut.
- Resow any damaged areas of grass.

In mid-spring:

- Plant out hardy annual bedding. Keep watered until established unless it rains.
- Plant out bare-root conifers and containerized plants.
- Plant up ponds except for deep aquatic plants.
- Prune early-flowering shrubs and climbers after flowering is over. (One-year-old shoots may not flower — if they do not, there is no need to prune.)

136

- Check for aphids and other pests. Spray if necessary.
- Continue mowing on slightly reduced cutting height.

In late spring:

- Support tall-growing plants.
- Start clipping vigorous hedges monthly.
- Sow hardy perennials and biennials now or in early summer.
- Cut down long grass where naturalized daffodils flowered.
- Continue checking for pests and diseases.
- Reduce cutting height of mower to final height (see p.73).
- Mulch warm, damp soil with ornamental mulch or leafmould.

THE NEW GARDEN

- Spread light-excluding mulches over ground to be cleared.
- Sow long-term green manures (see p.39).
- Dig in overwintered green manures at least two weeks prior to planting.
- Try to complete all planting of hardy plants.
- Start making compost or filling worm bins.
- Order manure to stack for next year.
- Thoroughly and regularly hoe and weed all planted areas.
- Sow new lawns.
- Keep all new plantings and sowings watered in dry weather.
- Mulch permanent plantings where possible once soil is warm.
- Where ground is prepared and ready for planting follow notes for established gardens (see above).
- Start mowing turfed lawns on a high cut, reducing cut through spring (see notes above). If cracks appear in turf brush in soil and sand mixture.

Summer

Now all your work starts to yield results. Vegetables fatten, fruits hang like jewels and bright flowers throng the borders. Home-grown produce starts to reach the kitchen.

GENERAL

- Keep plots weeded.
- Water in dry weather if it is needed.
- Remember to look after your worms in the worm bin. Keep contents moist and stand bin in the shade.
- Fill compost bins and turn contents as necessary.
- Sow green manures on vacant land between crops or to overwinter.

VEGETABLES AND FRUIT

In early summer:

- Support peas with netting or peasticks.
- Tie in tomatoes as they grow and remove sideshoots. Pinch out tops at end of July or early in August.
- Plant out leeks, kale and other late vegetables.
- Continue sowing late crops and successional lettuces.
- Harvest fruit and vegetables when ready, e.g. peas, beans, early potatoes, salads, strawberries, raspberries, gooseberries, blackcurrants.
- Lift shallots and leave to dry.
- Summer prune gooseberries and redcurrants.
- Pinch back shoots on wall-trained plums.
- When strawberries have finished fruiting, cut off old foliage and all runners.
- Continue checking regularly for pests and diseases.

In mid-summer:

- Carry out sowings for winter or overwintering crops.
- Lift garlic and leave to dry.
- Continue to harvest fruit and vegetables.
- Continue to remove runners on strawberries.
- Remove strawberry plants that have cropped for three

years and compost them. Prepare a new bed elsewhere and order crowns.

- Cut out fruited raspberry canes when crop is all harvested. Thin and tie in new canes.
- Tie in growing blackberries and hybrid berries. Cut out fruited canes of hybrid berries after harvest.
- Prune apples and pears (cordons, espaliers, pyramids).
- Check for pests and diseases, especially caterpillars on cabbage family plants and blight on potatoes.

In late summer:

- Sow grazing rye on cleared plots to overwinter as green manure.
- Sow spring cabbage and hardy lettuce.
- Remove potato haulms early if attacked by blight.
- Lift maincrop potatoes on a dry day for storing.
- Lift onions and leave to dry. Store in nets when dry.
- Protect tender crops with cloches where practicable to avoid early frost damage.
- Continue harvesting fruit and vegetables.
- Cut out old canes of raspberries, hybrid berries and blackberries after fruiting. Tie in new canes.
- Plant out new strawberry crowns or pot up for later planting out if not ready.
- Prune wall-trained plums and sweet cherries, also blackcurrants, and complete summer pruning of apples and pears (cordons, espaliers and pyramids).
- Pick apples and pears when ripe.
- Check for caterpillars on cabbages and related plants.

TREES, SHRUBS, FLOWERS AND LAWNS
In early summer:

- Plant out remaining tender plants.
- Complete sowing of biennials and hardy perennials.
- Prick out biennial seedlings sown indoors.
- Trim back flowerheads and old foliage on herbaceous plants that have finished flowering.

- Cut hedges as necessary.
- Keep picking sweet peas to prolong flowering.
- Remove dead heads on roses unless of the type with ornamental hips.
- Keep ponds topped up. Plant deep-water aquatic plants.
- Mow lawns as needed but not if weather is too dry for growth.

In mid-summer:

- Move indoor-grown biennials and perennials outside in trays or pots to grow on.
- Transplant biennials (e.g. wallflowers, sweet Williams, Canterbury bells etc.) from outdoor seedbeds to waiting rows. Keep well watered.
- Plant autumn-flowering bulbs.
- Trim hedges as necessary.
- Remove dead heads on hybrid tea and other repeat-flowering roses but not those with ornamental hips.
- Keep picking sweet peas.
- Keep ponds topped up.

In late summer:

- Trim back summer-flowering heaths and heathers lightly with shears after flowering.
- Continue to trim vigorous hedges as necessary.
- Trim back flowerheads on herbaceous plants when flowering is completed. Leave some seedheads for birds.
- Continue picking sweet peas.
- Continue dead-heading of roses.
- Keep ponds topped up.
- Continue mowing if necessary.

THE NEW GARDEN

- Keep new plantings watered in long dry spells.
- Avoid doing any new planting if weather is hot and dry. It is better to wait until autumn.

- Hoe or dig out weeds regularly.

- No hedge pruning or clipping should be necessary in the first year. Vigorous hedges in their second year will need to have their sides but not their growing point trimmed (see p.101).

- Continue with unfinished landscaping work. Remember that concrete dries quite quickly in warm weather.

- Start mowing new lawns grown from seed when grass is long enough (see p.105).

- New turfed lawns can be mowed as normal but avoid cutting during long dry spells.

- Follow appropriate notes for established gardens.

Autumn

The garden slips gently to bed, giving us a final bounty for the kitchen and yielding its clothing to the earth in a glow of reds and browns. Plants with fine autumn colouring become the major features of the garden. It is a time for harvesting and storing and for tidying — with restraint.

GENERAL

- Tidy up in the garden as flowers fade and frost cuts down tender plants. Don't be too tidy: many birds feed on seeds from flowerheads and in late autumn hedgehogs will be looking for piles of leaves or debris for a hibernation site.

- Rake up leaves and stack for leafmould.

- Shred tough stems and compost all plant residues cleared from beds and borders.

- Burn any very tough or diseased material but check for hedgehogs before setting light to the pile (p.82).

- Prepare ground for winter.

VEGETABLES AND FRUIT

In early autumn:

- Lift maincrop potatoes, if not done already, on a dry day. Allow to dry and store in paper or hessian sacks.

- Complete lifting of seed-grown onions. Dry bulbs thoroughly before storing in nets or strung into ropes.
- Bring in any remaining green tomatoes to ripen.
- Lift and store beetroots, some carrots, turnips and other roots.
- Protect celeriac, swedes and remaining carrots with straw *in situ*.
- Dig plots and spread manure, leafmould or lime where appropriate.
- Continue to sow grazing rye on vacant land, manuring beforehand if necessary.
- Plant out spring cabbage, garlic, autumn onion sets.
- Broad beans and early peas can be sown outdoors but may do better if sown indoors in late winter.
- Lift and divide herbaceous herbs such as mint and tarragon.
- Continue harvesting late blackberries. Pick apples and pears for storing.
- Apply greasebands to apple and pear trees before the end of October.
- Cut down fruited canes of blackberries and complete tying-in of new canes.
- Plant out pot-grown strawberries.

In mid-autumn:

- Clear away crop remains promptly to compost bins.
- Cut down Jerusalem artichoke stalks. Shred or chop.
- Complete digging, manuring and liming. Winter field beans can be sown as green manure on remaining vacant land – but keep to rotation (see p.45).
- Plant out garlic if not done already.
- Lift celeriac, swedes and, in colder areas, carrots. Store.
- Pick remaining apples and store.
- Start planting out of new fruit bushes, trees or canes.
- Clear away straw round strawberries to compost heap

142

with any old, dead leaves.

- Remove fruit netting.

In late autumn:

- Lift and store celeriac, swedes and carrots if not done already. In milder districts carrots can be left out under straw through the winter.
- Lift a few parsnips and leeks in case hard frost prevents harvesting later.
- Check through stored fruit and vegetables.
- Plant out bare-root or containerized fruit bushes, trees or canes.
- Winter-prune apples, pears, gooseberries, redcurrants after leaves have fallen.
- Clear away fallen leaves to prevent spread of disease.
- Check that greasebands are still tacky and renew if necessary.
- Net gooseberry and currant bushes to protect from sparrows and bullfinches.

TREES, SHRUBS, FLOWERS AND LAWNS

In early autumn:

- Give final trim to hedges including native hedgerows.
- Plant out spring-flowering bulbs.
- Remove and compost frosted half-hardy annuals.
- Start lawncare programme (see p.75).
- Raise height of cut on mower.
- Repair patches of bare lawn with seed.
- Prune climbing and rambling roses.

In mid-autumn:

- Clear away dead annuals to compost heap.
- Rake up accumulations of leaves and make leaf heap.
- Tidy up flowerbeds but leave seedheads for birds. Dress beds with leafmould or compost as appropriate.
- Mow for the last time. Clean mower and arrange for servicing.
- Top-dress lawn on a dry day.

- Lift and divide herbaceous perennials that have outgrown their space.
- Lift tender perennials and bulbs and store in frost-free place over winter.
- Plant out biennials.
- Clear summer flowers from containers and pots on terraces and replace with spring bulbs and hardy plants to overwinter.
- Plant out container-grown shrubs and trees.
- Returf areas of damaged lawn.

In late autumn:

- Clear away remaining annuals to compost and complete tidying and manuring of beds.
- Rake up leaves and stack in leaf heap.
- Plant out bare-rooted deciduous trees and shrubs.
- Cut back stems of hybrid tea roses.
- Continue laying turf if necessary.
- Start new landscaping projects.

THE NEW GARDEN

- Clear away rubbish and cut down tall weed growth.
- Plan the garden.
- If you have decided what to plant, make your selection from garden centres or order by post.
- Start laying out beds.
- Start major landscaping work.
- In early autumn, lift ground-clearance mulches and either sow a green manure or prepare and plant up.
- New lawns: prepare and either sow in September or start laying turf from late autumn.
- For gardens started the previous year, see notes for established gardens.

Appendix 1
PLANTS FOR BEGINNERS

Understanding Latin Names

A SINGLE PLANT MAY have many names, not only worldwide but even within the same country. To ensure that any plant can be accurately identified in a commonly understood international language, a system of Latin names is used. The beginner gardener does not need to know all the ramifications of plant naming, but this simplified explanation may help in finding plants in catalogues or at garden centres.

All plants belong to *families* (see *Crop Rotations* p.45). These are subdivided into *genera* which are further divided into *species*. The *genus* and *species* provide a two-part name that identifies a particular plant, e.g.

(genus)	(species)	
Lonicera	*periclymenum*	(honeysuckle)

Variations to species occur in nature and also have been produced by the efforts of plant breeders. A further word or words (either in Latin or English) will then occur in the name, e.g.

Lonicera periclymenum "Serotina"

This is the cultivar "Serotina" of common honeysuckle — botanically similar but much more exotic in flower than the common species.

Note: An "x" in the name (e.g. *Magnolia* x *soulangiana*) indicates that the plant is a hybrid between two species (or very occasionally two genera).

The inclusion of plants in the following lists does not indicate that they require *no* effort or management to grow, but simply that they do not need special skills or techniques.

All plants will respond to care and attention. The lists are by no means extensive or all-inclusive but have been compiled to give the beginner some suggestions for filling the blank sheet of a new garden.

Vegetables

An asterisk (★) indicates that this vegetable should be started into life indoors.

Artichokes, Globe (buy plants)

Artichokes, Jerusalem

Beans, broad

★Beans, French and runner

Beetroot

Brassicas: cabbage, Brussels sprouts, broccoli, kale

Chard

Chicory

★Courgettes, marrows and **pumpkins**

Kohlrabi

Leeks

Onions (from sets)

Parsnips

Radishes

Salsify and **scorzonera**

Spinach and **spinach beet** (perpetual spinach)

Swedes

★Sweetcorn

Turnips

Fruit

There are some skills involved in successful fruit growing but beginners should not be put off by this. Fruit trees and bushes can produce good crops without maintenance but careful pruning will always improve the quality and consistency of fruiting.

Raspberries, blackberries and **hybrid berries** require strong supports, but you will find that pruning and training are relatively simple.

The easiest **apples** to grow are the modern "Ballerina" varieties that require virtually no pruning at all.

It may prove sensible to start with strawberries and experiment in successive years with other fruit, so that skills are acquired slowly.

Ornamental Plants

FLOWERING ANNUALS AND BIENNIALS

All *hardy* annuals and biennials are quite easy to care for. Half-hardy annuals require early sowing in guaranteed warmth. If you cannot provide this, do not attempt them. Alternatively buy plants from a reputable source in late spring.

Plants will only grow well in conditions that suit them. The plants suggested below have been divided into groups corresponding either to their type or to their preferred growing conditions: e.g. shade, full sun, acid soil etc. In the lists of trees and shrubs, the letters 'D' and 'E' stand for 'Deciduous' and 'Evergreen' respectively.

PLANTS FOR ACID SOILS

Trees and Shrubs:

Plant	(D/E)	Max. ht. or habit	Special interest
Abies koreana	E (conifer)	9 m	ornamental cones
Acer palmatum "Dissectum"	D	2.5 m	autumn colour
Amelanchier canadensis	D	5.5 m	spring flowers
Calluna vulgaris (heaths)	E	ground cover	flowers and foliage
Cornus kousa	D	7.5 m	flower bracts and autumn colour
Corylopsis pauciflora	D	2 m	spring flowers: autumn colour
Cryptomeria japonica "Vilmoriniana"	E (conifer)	90 cm	foliage
Erica, most species (heather)	E	mostly ground cover	flowers
Fothergilla monticola	D	2.4m	fragrant flowers, autumn colour (needs light shade)
Hamamelis mollis	D	3.5 m	fragrant winter flowers
Magnolia stellata	D	3 m	fragrant spring flowers
Parotia persica	D	5.5 m	autumn colour
Picea glauca albertiana 'Conica'	E (conifer)	3 m	foliage

Rhododendrons of all types including azaleas

147

Other perennials:

Plant	Flower colour	Height	Season
Gentiana sino-ornata	blue	15 cm	autumn
Lilium davidii	red/orange	1-1.4m	summer
Lilium tigrinum	orange	1.5 m	summer/autumn
Liriope muscari	violet	45 cm	summer/autumn
Lupinus "Russell Hybrids"	mixed	1.2 m	spring/summer
Meconopsis betonicifolia	blue	1.5 m	summer
Primula vulgaris (primrose)	yellow	15 cm	spring
Primula vulgaris elatior	mixed	30 cm	spring
Trillium grandiflorum	white	45 cm	spring (needs light shade)

PLANTS FOR ALKALINE AND SHALLOW, CHALKY SOILS

Trees and Shrubs:

Plant	(D/E)	Max. ht. or habit	Special interest
Buddleia davidii	D	2-3 m, if pruned	fragrant flowers
Cercis siliquastrum	D	7 m	flowers and fruit
Clematis, all types	D	climber	flowers
Daphne mezereum	D	1.5 m	early fragrant flowers
Erica carnea (heather)	E	ground cover	winter flowers
Helianthemum nummularium	E	20–25 cm	flowers all summer
Osmanthus delavayi	E	2.5 m	fragrant flowers (not fully hardy)
Prunus "Kiku-shidare Sakura"	D	6 m	spring flowers
Syringa vulgaris (choose named cultivars)	D	3 m	fragrant flowers

Other perennials:

Plant	Flower colour	Height	Season
Anthemis cupaniana	large white daisy	30 cm	summer
Aubrietia deltoidea	violet	15 cm; ground cover	spring
Campanula cochlearifolia	pale blue	10 cm	summer
Dianthus plumarius "Mrs Sinkins"	pink	30 cm	summer

Iris germanica	various	90 cm	June
Linaria purpurea	pink	90 cm	summer/autumn (heavy soils)
Papaver orientale (poppy)	orange/red	75 cm	spring/summer
Primula veris (cowslip)	yellow	15 cm	late spring
Pulsatilla vulgaris	purple	30 cm	spring
Salvia x superba	purple	90 cm	summer/autumn
Saxifraga umbrosa	pink	30 cm	spring/autumn (best in damp shade)
Scabiosa caucasica	various	75 cm	summer/autumn
Sedum spectabile	pink/red	45 cm	late summer/autumn
Thymus vulgaris (thyme)	lilac	20 cm	summer
Verbascum bombyciferum	yellow	up to 1.8 m	mid-summer

PLANTS FOR CLAY SOILS

Trees and Shrubs:

Plant	(D/E)	Max. ht. or habit	Special interest
Aucuba japonica	E	2.4 m	foliage
Chaenomeles speciosa	D	2.4 m	flowers and fruits
Cornus alba "Spaethii"	D	2.4 m	stems in winter; flowers and foliage; autumn colour
Crataegus oxyacantha (hawthorn)	D	6 m	flowers and fruit
Forsythia x intermedia	D	2.4 m	yellow spring flowers
Hedera helix (ivy)	E	ground cover or climbing	foliage
Magnolia x soulangiana	D	4.5 m	flowers
Pieris floribunda	E	1.8 m	flowers (acid soil)
Ribes sanguineum	D	1.8 m	flowers
Salix daphnoides	D	9 m	flowers and twigs
Spiraea x arguta	D	2.4 m	flowers
Viburnum plicatum	D	2.4 m; spreading	flowers; autumn colour
Weigela florida	D	1.8 m	flowers

Other perennials:

Plant	Flower colour	Height	Season
Anemone japonica	white	1 m	autumn
Aster novi-belgii "Audrey" (Michaelmas daisy)	pale blue	45 cm	autumn

149

Crocosmia masonorum	orange/red	75 cm	late summer
Doronicum plantagineum	yellow	75 cm	spring/summer
Helenium autumnale			
"Coppelia"	copper	90 cm	summer
Lysimachia clethroides	white	90 cm	summer/autumn
Monarda didyma	scarlet	90 cm	summer
Narcissus (daffodil)	yellow	30-45 cm	spring
Polygonum affine	red/pink	25 cm	summer/autumn
Rudbeckia fulgida	yellow	60 cm	summer/autumn
"Goldsturm"	daisy		

PLANTS FOR SHADY PLACES

Most of these plants will tolerate fairly dry conditions.

Shrubs:

Plant	(D/E)	Max. ht. or habit	Special interest
Aucuba japonica	E	2.4 m	foliage (and berries, if male and female planted)
Cornus canadensis	D	15 cm; ground cover	flowers and foliage
Gaultheria shallon	E	1.8 m	flowers and berries (acid soils only)
Hypericum calycinum	D/E	45 cm; ground cover	yellow flowers
Hydrangea macrophylla "Nikko Blue"	D	1.5 m	blue flowers
Mahonia aquifolium	E	1.2 m; suckering	flowers and berries
Pachysandra terminalis	E	ground cover	fragrant flowers (acid soils only)
Rubus tricolor	E	ground cover	foliage
Ruscus aculeatus	E	90 cm	berries (if male and female planted)
Sarcococca humilis	E	60 cm	fragrant flowers
Vinca major and V. minor	E	ground cover	flowers and foliage

Other perennials:

Plant	Flower colour	Height	Season
Convallaria majalis	white	20 cm	spring
Cyclamen neapolitanum	pink	15 cm	summer/autumn

Dicentra eximia	pink	40 cm	spring/summer/ autumn
Dryopteris filix-mas (fern)	—	120 cm	foliage all year
Epimedium x rubrum	red/white	30 cm	spring
Euphorbia robbiae	green	60 cm	spring/summer
Liriope muscari	violet	45 cm	summer/autumn
Polypodium vulgare (fern)	—	30 cm	foliage all year
Tellima grandiflora	pale green	60 cm	spring/summer

CLIMBERS FOR EAST AND NORTH-FACING WALLS

Plant	Max. ht.	Spread	Flower colour	Season
Celastrus orbiculatus	12 m	5.5 m	green	autumn for leaf colour and berries
Hedera helix (many varieties)	30 m	5.5 m	—	foliage all year
Hedera colchica (many varieties)	12 m	6 m	—	foliage all year
Hydrangea petiolaris	24 m	6 m	white	June
Lonicera periclymenum "Serotina" (honeysuckle)	3.5 m	3.5 m	red, purple and yellow; fragrant	summer/autumn
Parthenocissus quinquefolia	9 m	9 m	—	autumn colour
Schizophragma integrifolia	12 m	5.5 m	white	July

CLIMBERS FOR WEST OR SOUTH-FACING WALLS

Plant	Max. ht.	Spread	Flower colour	Season
Actinidia kolomikta	5 m	4 m	white	June
Campsis radicans	12 m	3 m	orange/red	summer/autumn
Clematis (many types — note pruning needed when buying)				
Jasminum officinale	9 m	6 m	white, fragrant	summer
Jasminum nudiflorum	3 m	3 m	yellow	winter/spring
Roses (many types)				summer
Solanum crispum "Glasnevin"	6 m	6 m	purple/yellow	summer (warm areas only)
Vitis vinifera "Brandt"	9 m	6 m	fruiting vine	autumn colour
Vitis coignetiae	21 m	12 m	inedible fruits	autumn colour
Wisteria sinensis	21 m	15 m	lilac, fragrant	late spring

COMMON HEDGING PLANTS

Native types:

Common name	Latin name	D/E	Wildlife use and visual interest
Alder buckthorn	Rhamnus frangula	D	berries
Common buckthorn	Rhamnus cathartica	D	berries
Beech	Fagus sylvatica	D	holds brown leaves in winter
Blackthorn	Prunus spinosa	D	fruits
Dog rose	Rosa canina	D	flowers and hips
Dogwood	Cornus sanguinea	D	autumn colour; fruits; red stems in winter
Guelder rose	Viburnum opulus	D	flowers; autumn colour; berries
Hazel	Corylus avellana	D	nuts
Hawthorn	Crataegus monogyna	D	berries (haws)
Holly	Ilex aquifolium	E	berries if male and female planted
Hornbeam	Carpinus betulus	D	holds dead leaves in winter
Hedge or field maple	Acer campestre	D	autumn colour
Oak, common	Quercus robur	D	acorns
Oak, sessile	Quercus petraea	D	acorns
Sweet briar	Rosa rubiginosa	D	flowers, hips
Spindle	Euonymus europaeus	D	flowers; pink berries
Wild privet	Ligustrum vulgare	Semi-E	berries
Yew	Taxus baccata	E	berries

OTHER HEDGING PLANTS:

Plant	D/E	Trim	Notes/Special interest
Buxus sempervirens (Box)	E	late summer	very slow-growing
Berberis x stenophylla	D	after flowering	yellow flowers in spring
Cupressocyparis leylandii	E	August	vigorous: quick screen
Chamaecyparis lawsoniana	E	August	vigorous: quick screen
Cotoneaster simonsii	Semi-E	July	loose, informal hedge, spring flowers, autumn berries
Elaeagnus x ebbingei	E	August	silver-grey foliage
Ligustrum ovalifolium "Aureum"	semi-E	May-August	golden foliage
Lonicera nitida	E	May-August	very fast-growing
Pyracantha rogersiana	E	June and August	clip lightly for good show of flowers and berries
Thuja plicata	E	August	fast-growing

Appendix 2
BOOK LIST

SOME SUGGESTIONS for further reading. You will not want to buy too many books. Many of the titles listed, especially the heftier reference books, will be available from your library.

FEEDING SOIL AND PLANTS

Algar, Chris *The Chase Organics Gardening Manual* (Ian Allan)

Kitto, Dick *Composting* (Thorsons)

Pears, Pauline *How to Make your Garden Fertile*, Organic Handbook Series No. 1 (HDRA/Search Press)

GROWING VEGETABLES AND FRUIT ORGANICALLY

Algar, Chris *The Chase Organics Manual of Fruit and Vegetable Cultivation* (Ian Allan)

Bullock, Rob, and Gould, Gillie *The Allotment Book* (Optima)

Hay, Jim *Vegetables Naturally* (Century Arrow)

Hills, Lawrence *Organic Gardening* (Penguin)

Hills, Lawrence *Month by Month Organic Gardening* (Thorsons)

Sherman, Bob, and Bowen, Carol *The Green Gardening and Cooking Guide* (Pan)

Stickland, Sue *Planning the Organic Herb Garden* (Thorsons)

Tolhurst, Iain *A Gardener's Guide to Growing Strawberries Organically*

GROWING ORNAMENTAL PLANTS ORGANICALLY

Chambers, John *Wild Flower Garden* (Hamlyn)

Gibbons, Bob and Liz *Creating a Wildlife Garden* (Hamlyn)

Stickland, Sue *Planning the Organic Flower Garden* (Thorsons)

GENERAL BOOKS ON ORGANIC GARDENING

Elphinstone, Margaret, and Langley, Julia *The Green Gardeners' Handbook* (Thorsons)

Hamilton, Geoff *Successful Organic Gardening* (Dorling Kindersley)

Step by Step Organic Gardening (HDRA) – a series of small booklets:

1. 'What is Organic Gardening?'
2. 'Composting'
3. 'Pest Control Without Poisons'
4. 'Making Worm Compost'
5. 'Mulching'
6. 'The Organic Lawn'
7. 'Growing from Seed'
8. 'Gardening for Wildlife'
9. 'Weed Control Without Chemicals'
10. 'On the Slug Trail'
11. 'Gardening with Green Manures'
12. 'Comfrey'

Stickland, Sue *The Organic Garden* (Hamlyn)

OTHER BOOKS OF GENERAL INTEREST

Bleasdale, J.K.A., Slater, P.J., and others *Know and Grow Vegetables*, Vols 1 and 2 (Oxford University Press)

Larkcom, Joy *Vegetables for Small Gardens* (Faber & Faber)

Larkcom, Joy *The Salad Garden* (Windward)

CONTROLLING PESTS AND DISEASES ORGANICALLY

Buczacki, Stefan, and Harris, Keith *Collins Guide to the Pests, Diseases and Disorders of Garden Plants* (Collins). Not organic, but very useful for identification of problems.

Chinery, Michael *Garden Creepy-Crawlies* (Whittet)

Sherman, Bob, and Pears, Pauline *How to Control Fruit and Vegetable Pests*, Organic Handbook Series No. 2 (HDRA/ Search Press)

PRUNING

Brickell, Christopher *RHS Encyclopaedia of Practical Gardening: Pruning* (Mitchell Beazley)

Brown, George E., *The Pruning of Trees, Shrubs and Conifers* (Faber & Faber)

GARDEN CONSTRUCTION AND DESIGN

Baines, Chris *How to Make a Wildlife Garden* (Elm Tree)

Farthing, Guy and Donald *Popular Garden Designs* (Foulsham)

Leverett, Brian *Garden Design − Planning Smaller Gardens* (Crowood Gardening Guides)

Titchmarsh, Alan *RHS Encyclopaedia of Practical Gardening: Gardening Techniques* (Mitchell Beazley)

CHOOSING AND FINDING PLANTS

RHS Gardeners' Encyclopaedia of Plants and Flowers (Dorling Kindersley)

Ferguson Nicola *Right Plant, Right Place* (Pan)

Johnson, Hugh, and Miles, Paul *The Mitchell Beazley Pocket Guide to Garden Plants* (Mitchell Beazley)

Philip, Chris *The Plant Finder* (Moorland)

Rice, Graham *Plants for Problem Places* (Christopher Helm)

Seabrook, Peter *Shrubs for Your Garden* (Floraprint)

Swindells, Philip *The Water Gardeners' Handbook* (Croom Helm)

Appendix 3
USEFUL SOCIETIES AND SUPPLIERS

ORGANIZATIONS

The Henry Doubleday Research Association (HDRA), National Centre for Organic Gardening, Ryton-on-Dunsmore, Coventry CV8 3LG. Tel: 0203 303517

A membership organization and the largest organic gardening society in Europe. One of very few organizations specializing in research into organic growing. Demonstration gardens open daily to the public.

The Soil Association, 86 Colston Street, Bristol BS1 5BB. Tel: 0272 290661

A membership organization, campaigning for and promoting organic methods of food production. Their symbol guarantees authenticity on products such as sprays, fertilizers and potting composts as well as food grown organically.

The Organic Advisory Service, Elm Farm Research Centre, Hampstead Marshall, Newbury, Berks RG15 0RH. Tel: 0635 254987

An advisory body for organic farmers and commercial growers. Also provides soil analysis service to organic gardeners.

Royal Horticultural Society, Vincent Square, London SW1P 2PE. Tel: 071 834 4334

Northern Horticultural Society, Harlow Carr Gardens, Crag Lane, Harrogate, Yorkshire HG3 1QB. Tel: 0423 565418

Royal Caledonian Horticultural Society, 3 West Newington Place, Edinburgh EH9 1QT.

Royal Horticultural Society of Ireland, Thomas Prior House, RDS, Merrion Road, Dublin 4. Tel: 0103531 684358

National Society of Allotment and Leisure Gardeners, Hunters Road, Corby, Northants NN17 1JE. Tel: 0536 66576

The Hardy Plant Society, 10 St Barnabas Road, Emmer Green, Caversham, Reading RG4 8RA

The Herb Society, 77 Great Peter Street, London SW1 1EZ

SUPPLIERS

The following businesses offer mail order, and, in some cases, shop facilities for the purchase of organic sundries.

Chase Organics (GB) Ltd, Coombelands House, Coombelands Lane, Addlestone, Weybridge KT15 1HY. Tel: 0932 858511

Seeds, books, potting composts, fertilizers, soil improvers and pest control products.

Cumulus Organics and Conservation Ltd, Two Mile Lane, Highnam, Glos GL2 8BR. Tel: 0452 305814

Potting composts, fertilizers, soil improvers, mulches, pest and weed control products and booklets.

HDRA (Sales) Ltd, National Centre for Organic Gardening, Ryton-on-Dunsmore, Coventry CV8 3LG. Tel: 0203 303517

Seeds, plants, books, leaflets, potting composts, fertilizers, soil improvers and mulches, compost bins, garden tools. (Shop and mail order.)

Centre for Alternative Technology, Maccynlleth, Powys SY20 9AZ. Tel: 0654 702400

Seeds, plants, books, leaflets, potting composts, fertilizers, compost bins, energy-efficient devices for the house and garden. (Demonstration garden and energy displays open to the public.)

Suffolk Herbs, Sawyers Farm, Little Cornard, Sudbury, Suffolk, CO10 0NY. Tel: 0787 227247

Seeds, herbs, books and some general garden sundries.

INDEX